Prison-wise

The Psychology of Incarceration, The Potential for Change

By Dr. Jack Jaffe
Chief of Psychology
Federal Correctional Institution
Federal Prisons

D1153706

Contents

Personal Disclaimer: Opinions expressed in this book are those of the author and do not necessarily represent opinions of the Federal Bureau of Prisons or the Department of Justice.

Forward

In <u>Prison-wise: The Psychology of Incarceration, The Potential for Change</u>, I discuss the internal world of inmates, the adjustments they must make, the institution of prisons, and reforms that are needed.

This book is not intended to present policies and procedures. It is also not a sanitized version of prisons. It is a frank discussion about what prisons are like, the impact it has on inmates, and realistic ways to reform the prisons. It was written for people concerned about crime rates, incarceration rates, and the ways it has affected individuals and their families. My outlook comes from 15 years of experience working in the prisons as a clinical psychologist, talking to and treating inmates. As with <u>There's no Crying in Prison</u>, while the names of institutions, individuals, and circumstances have been changed to protect the identity of the individuals who work and live here, it's a factual account. As for the events described, I personally witnessed them. The few exceptions that were relayed to me by others are identified as such.

I hope this book will be read by students of criminal justice, correctional staff, inmates and their families, and especially the general public. Perhaps it will provide a spark so that more people will advocate for creating improved prisons. Ultimately, I would like to see ex-felons have the opportunity to reenter society better prepared to become lasting contributors.

Acknowledgements

As with my first book, **There's No Crying in Prison**, I thank my family for their patience and support while I wrote the book. Phyllis Newton assisted with editorial and administrative tasks. Dr. Robert Denney and Dr. Stanton Samenow, both of whom are published psychologists, provided professional guidance. Hollie Relethford served as my editor. Tonya Klar verified and typed references.

I appreciate this federal agency where I have learned about corrections and the staff who taught me about working in a prison. There are many individuals with whom I've served alongside these many years who I want to acknowledge. They kept me safe inside these prison walls as I have them. I also want to recognize and thank the many inmates who have shared their insights and understanding of prison with me. Lastly, I appreciate my colleagues in Psychology whose knowledge and clinical skill in the performance of their duties has contributed to my own.

Chapter 1

Busted: The Experience of Incarceration

"Prison is no fairy tale world."
Red, in <u>Shawshank Redemption</u>

Freedom to Felon

You needn't be at the crime scene to get caught. The police can reach out and grab you years after the offense. Some who led a life of crime go straight- they try to leave it behind them. But the paper trail, the witnesses, and the co-conspirators don't go away so easily. You remain vulnerable for many years after the criminal conduct. Federal authorities might have been building a case without the accused ever knowing they were under investigation. Your name could have come up years after you left your criminal life behind you. They can pick you up anywhere. Individuals report being arrested while driving on the interstate, half asleep in their bedrooms, at the grocery store, or working at their jobs. Computers, laptops, files, and cell phones get seized, cars get impounded. With a public arrest, there is a public humiliation: then, the dread of having to call home to tell your loved one you're in jail. Or you're busted at home while your family watches you forced to the floor, handcuffed, and carted off to the police station.

Newly arrested men at the jail are often in a panic. They want to call their wives to inform them they are not coming home from the grocery store. They want to tell their children "goodbye" or "I'm sorry" or offer an explanation before it hits the nightly news. If they ask for sympathy from the processing officers to make a phone call, they might hear, "You should have thought of that beforehand." There is no access to phones yet: their only contact is with other arrestees. Their companions might be twenty other guys sitting with them on a concrete bench in a holding cell. They are crowded together with their cuffs on, thinking about the family finances, their wife having to pay the bills, managing the kids, and all the other ongoing family issues. They wonder if she will ask for a divorce. They worry about the family shame, what people will say. They are wondering if they can come up with enough money for a lawyer. They are digging up alibis and explanations, trying to sort out who knows what and how they got caught. We might think they should have planned for these contingencies before they arrived at our facility. For them it is a frantic moment, with despair and helplessness.

While the initial arrest might come as a shock, if you have been charged by the feds you should anticipate incarceration. The Department of Justice report high conviction rates, in some cases as high as 98%.[1] If you are smart, you plead out, admit to your illegal actions, inform on all your friends and co-conspirators, and hope for the shortest sentence possible. Once convicted, you self-surrender. You can't ignore the self-surrender paperwork because you will be re-arrested and face additional charges. If you flee, you will eventually get caught because authorities know your family and your contacts, have your fingerprints, photographs, and DNA, and have an international police network ready to track you down. Inmates out on bond after sentencing drive up to the prison gates with their family, say their goodbyes, and walk into the prison suitcase in hand, ready for the start of their incarceration. The look on their faces captured in mug shots shows the bitter pill it is.

Stressors from going to prison

What are the major stressors in life? I researched as many as I could find on the internet. Most of them become activated when incarcerated. They are listed below in alphabetical order:

-Career change, change in routine, crowding, cultural confusion, divorce or separation, family tension, financial difficulties, frustrated expectations, lack of access to a natural environment, lack of personal control, loss of family support, loss of possessions, moving, noise levels, perceived inequality, reduced access to immediate medical care, social exclusion, social tension, sustained personal criticism, threats to personal safety, time pressure (e.g., filing deadlines), and unemployment (e.g., being idle).

The impact of being in prison is a major psychological assault. I would argue that of all human errors, there is hardly a more tragic one than criminal irresponsibility.

The First Day of Jail

Inmates tell me the shock of incarceration usually comes quickly. The physical environment dominates: the steel handcuffs and shackles, the heavy door slamming, hearing the lock slide, seeing the fences with concertina wire. The environment is stark: long, narrow hallways, sterile cells, cinderblock walls, concrete floors. They think, "This is it. I can't get out". The world got hard and they got small. They are numb. Brought to the housing units, it is now time to absorb the social environment. The sea of inmate faces, the variety of races, the sounds of other languages, and the realization they are alone among many.

After the shock lifts, before they find their way, most inmates initially experience fear. Even the big guys who know how to fight feel it. Someone might challenge them, everyone wants to measure them. An inmate tells me that they come at you in so many ways, testing you, seeing what you are made of- so much so that they can precisely score you on a scale of 1 to 10 within hours of your arrival. This is their science. They play with the younger guys- maybe telling them they have to fight right away to establish themselves. They tell him to fashion a knife and go after someone. Then they laugh at the results. They threaten the older guys, make bogus charges- claim they were disrespected, they were brushed into, their property was kicked, or their mattress was stepped on. They want apologies. You have to answer to them- not frightened, not aggressive, not subservient, but even. The whole cell gets ranked and everyone knows just where they stand until the new guy comes in and the deck gets reshuffled. The first night they won't sleep.

The First Week of Jail

Imagine the lives of men for the first week of incarceration if they couldn't post bond, prior to conviction, while awaiting court. The transformation is total. The life they knew is gone. They are unprepared for what awaits them. They have no family around and no friends. They initially don't have access to phones, letters, and visits. They are living among strangers they presume are criminals. They are being tested. They are possibly being disrespected, taunted, and threatened. Guards at this time are a faceless, possibly rough and rude, bureaucratic. They are being processed into the system, fingerprinted, photographed, stripped, re-clothed, and directed. Their secrets are documented and known by strangers who manage them. Their body has been scrutinized and all of their distinguishing characteristics photographed. Legally presumed innocent, they are treated no differently than the convicted and in that sense presumed to be criminals, too.

Their new role is to be an inmate. They cannot complain without getting criticized or ignored. They are subjected to crowding and there is no privacy. They use public bathrooms. They see only concrete and bars during the day, or perhaps they get a narrow window view of barbed wire fence and more buildings. Noise levels are high. They get instructions through a loud, static-filled intercom system. There is an echo in enclosed spaces. They hear cat-calls, yelling, men laughing loudly. They are told "rack up," "wait for count," "do a cop-out," and other slang they won't know. They must mimic others to stay in line. They must fit all their possessions into a tiny locker. They don't choose their routines. The food is bland institutional served directly on molded plastic trays. The lights are bright. There is nothing to do with their time or, alternately, lots of filing deadlines and legal paperwork they have a rough time tracking. The dizzying transformation from citizen to prisoner is radical and all encompassing.

The First Few Months of Incarceration

"At the penitentiary, I saw a young guy's hair go from black to white in six months" an inmate told me. Those who have already done time might see it as "just another incarceration" but for the new inmate it's frightening. When the terror subsides to "within normal limits" you can live with the daily fear. One inmate told me, "There are a lot of ways things can go wrong for you every day. You got to be careful but something can still happen."

After the fear, there is misery. Pain, suffering, longing, sadness, depression, and grief are all a part of the mix. The losses are extensive. A person's life script has to be re-written from being an integrated societal member to being an outcast. There is shame. Friends write in the beginning but soon stop. Family members initially visit to be assured that you are safe but then peel away. Your job, house, neighborhood, and community are now gone. One man described feeling as if he already died, that he was living on a cloud, and could just helplessly watch his family go on about their lives without him. There is no one there for you when you are hurt or when you are ill. You have no cash, no autonomy, and no freedom. You have to rebuild your life from the bottom up. You have to take stock in what you do have and try to make that enough to keep going. Accept all that you've lost- both the tangible and intangible. Try to find some kind of inner strength, some kind of will to continue.

Inmates miss different things, sometimes very mundane. They long for good music, petting their dog, a loved one's cooking, certain foods, washing their car, a pipe, or the taste of tobacco. They long for privacy, to hear their own thoughts. Inmates cry openly about missing their families. Those who have been through divorce cry about not being able to hug their kids. It's virtually impossible to force a divorced wife, even through the courts, to bring their children to a prison if she doesn't want to. The pain can be a constant presence during their incarceration- they just learn to live with it. Many men ask family not to visit because each new separation re-opens the wounds.

There is often rage during the incarceration though the target varies- the informant who snitched, the family who abandoned them, the ex-wife who keeps them from their kids, the parents who never paid attention, the prosecutor for the dirty dealing, the police for the insults, the prison staff for its callous mistreatment, the judge for the length of the sentence, themselves for being greedy, criminal, addicted, or stupid, the probation office for not giving them a chance, and society for not giving them a decent job. Many are particularly bitter at the prosecutors and police whom, they believe, played dirty. They don't so much argue that they weren't guilty but complain that they were lied to or that false evidence was used against them. Some inmates fantasize about revenge against the law enforcement people who got them here, some against family. One inmate reports that he has always worshipped Satan and spends his time praying for the death of his parents for the abuse he suffered at their hands. Inmates who we think might credibly carry out their threats are sent back to the courts to postpone their release from prison through civil commitment.

The First Few Years

Inmates were formerly free citizens who were treated with respect and equality. It is shocking for many to experience how stark the power difference is between inmate and guard. If their two-man room gets cited during inspection, they are told by the officer to move their stuff to the twenty-man day room amid laughs and cat-calls from the other inmates. They aren't used to being talked to so bluntly without recourse. They might be seated at a table reading a newspaper and told, "Get out, beat it," and be forced to leave by a tough officer. Some men develop a subservient attitude and start calling officers "Boss man." I remember a medical doctor in his former life who deteriorated under these conditions. He entered the prison relatively self-confident but gradually turned inward. There was no single event but he succumbed to the daily grind of rough prison life and eventually lost contact with that fragile sense of pride the rest of us take for granted. Toward the end of his incarceration, he would just look down on the ground, saying "yes, sir" and "no, sir" without prompting, having become an isolated, damaged man. The transition from highly respected man of the community to lowly inmate had broken him.

Inmates find it difficult to establish their identity in a prison. It's compounded when we don't remember their names. Eight-digit numbers are easier for computer searches and are pasted onto every shirt and pair of pants they wear, so their individuality gets lost. They are counted by staff five times per day where they are literally just numbers to us. People have a basic need for identity so many inmates find alternate ways to identify themselves. They might imperceptibly alter their clothes with distinct creases or the movement of buttons. Some guys go tattoo crazy, entering prison clean but leaving completely inked. Others become attached to their bibles, their cells, or their desks. They carve a quote somewhere or keep hidden some personal item that has meaning; a photograph, a small gift, or a carving. It becomes their talisman, losing it can be traumatic.

In addition to the constraints on identity, inmates have no choice but to live with the restrictions of an "us vs. them world." Their interactions with staff are observed by other inmates and if it appears too chummy they can expect trouble. Many inmates avoid staff because we represent the evil government that incarcerated them. Those who are still looking to beat the system might develop a cat and mouse relationship with us. They keep their distance to avoid getting caught while involved in their games and scams. Regardless, the end result is that the relationship between staff and inmates is essentially of two separate entities working in parallel. By keeping expectations for interaction low, there is less chance for conflict and disappointment. Staff members have the same mindset. We're all doing time together with no reason to add problems. I remember one inmate appealing the denial of a medical procedure observing, "You staff are all team players. One of you lies and all the others swear by it. I hoped you doctors would come through for me but you are property of this agency like everyone else and I don't stand a chance." That's not a fully accurate criticism but certainly understandable. While we provide services, we do so with a bureaucratic objectivity that can be experienced as cold-hearted. Misinterpretations abound.

When inmates come to the Psychology Department for

help, we ask them to sign a confidentiality statement just as they do in the free world but with one big difference. In the free world they are essentially being promised confidentiality. In the prison we are advising them that we share their information. The document is not so much a confidentiality form as a "Limits to Confidentiality" form. Inmates start realizing that much of what they say is tracked by staff and can be communicated about openly. Although we try to be discrete for their benefit, some suspect that psychology too is caught up in the dichotomous world of "us vs. them."

The Last Few Years

Once inmates have adapted to prison and are approaching release, a concern is that they have become "institutionalized," which is to say they have acculturated so much to the institution that they won't be able to successfully return to society. Although not likely to remain a problem post incarceration, inmates towards the end of their sentence may have become more passive, expecting others to direct them rather than initiating activity themselves. Or perhaps they've become more vigilant and suspicious in their interactions, less trusting of others and more doubtful about what they are told. They may have adopted a stoic, tough exterior to keep others distant while feeling emotionally isolated. Or they have developed feelings of being inferior and lack confidence in their ability to succeed. Perhaps they are more tolerant of a criminal sub-culture and have learned to "look the other way" when there are problems. Or they avoid others altogether for fear of getting into trouble. The converse can also be a problem should they feel embittered by their incarceration with plans to take it out on others after they release. That's why it's not realistic to assume we can "just throw away the key" after a man gets locked up. Eventually he is coming back out. It's in our interest to prepare inmates to become functioning, contributing members of society.

Chapter 2

Mental Health Issues in Prison

"To live without hope is to cease to live."
Fyodor Dostoevsky

In many ways, psychology services play a peripheral role in a prison. We are not part of the constant monitoring, directing, and controlling functions of the correctional staff. We can influence staff to make exceptions for severely mentally ill inmates but for the most part we use that privilege sparingly for fear that it will be abused. We can't protect inmates from the realities of prison life. We also can't force inmates to make personal changes the way an officer forces an inmate to go to his cell, make his bed, or accept a pat search. We don't direct large groups of inmates to the dining hall at meal time or to the factory for work. We generally don't lock inmates up for insolence or search through their cells for contraband. Our function is more often to educate, persuade, treat, reassure and encourage. We tend to work with individuals or small groups rather than large groups- often with people who are marginalized within the institution. We primarily use communication to influence events. Our efforts are to get people to learn better techniques of social communication; accept different perspectives; think through their actions; and try out new behaviors. Our power comes from the power of our message.

We still pride ourselves on making a significant contribution to the safe and orderly running of the institution.

A large institution cannot operate with residents who are not following directions, are too anxious to perform properly, or who need more attention than a busy officer can provide. In that sense, just as with officers, we are keeping the machinery of the place properly operating by making sure that the outliers, who would otherwise be disruptive, are being attended to and, ultimately, are falling into line.

The mentally ill

About 45% of the inmate population has a diagnosable mental illness during at least some part of their incarceration.[2] Most of them, approximately 30% of the inmate population, have symptoms consistent with mild to moderate problems with mental health, sometimes temporary adjustment problems. This would include problems such as anxiety, depression, traumatic stress responses, sleep difficulties, and emotional self regulation. That leaves about 15% with significant mental illness including disorders such as schizophrenia, psychosis, major depression, and bipolar disorder.[3] These are chronic conditions that periodically worsen or improve but rarely remit during an incarceration. Psychologists in the prisons focus more on these severely mentally ill due to limited staff resources. They are the most in need and the most disruptive. Inmates with fewer problems might get brief adjustment counseling but little else.

Those with character pathology generally aren't offered treatment at all nor are they interested. They avoid psychologists because it advertises weakness or confronts them with having to change. Since their motivation is low, so is our chance of success. They need intensive treatment programs to address criminal thinking but there isn't sufficient staff time for that. They might go their entire incarceration without a single contact with psychology other than the obligatory intake interview.

People don't always understand that inmates can be both severely mentally ill in their functioning and criminal in their outlook. The two diagnoses are not mutually exclusive. Mental illness does not necessarily cause or even contribute to their criminal behavior. Men can hear voices, have manic episodes, feel paranoid and frightened, hold delusional ideas, and struggle to comply with medication regimens while at the same time practice thievery, robbery, and drug dealing to earn a living. There is no clear boundary between "unfortunate soul" and "predatory criminal." They inhabit the same body and so we go back and forth in our own emotional reactions to them, sometimes concerned for them due to their vulnerabilities and at other times frightened by their criminal potential. While I have never yet been assaulted in a prison, the closest I ever came was with a mentally ill inmate who misinterpreted a remark I made. He literally jumped out of his chair, put his face up in mine, and clenched both hands ready to strike. Fortunately, I was able to calm him down while alerting correctional officers who restrained him.

Not everyone is so lucky. There are many tragic cases of psychologists who have been assaulted by the inmates they were attempting to treat. As in the real world, the mentally ill oftentimes deny their illness and refuse their medications. Many don't comply because they hate the side effects. They may be reluctant to be perceived as "crazy" or may not accept that they are mentally ill. Others prefer the fantasy world of their illness to the constraints of reality. As a result, psychologists here are frequently tasked with the unpleasant job of convincing angry inmates to comply with an officer's directives or a psychiatrist's prescriptions. When the inmate is actively psychotic and aggressive, there is no substitute for medication to calm them down and keeping them in a locked cell where they won't hurt anybody. Counseling in such circumstances won't be sufficient. I've participated in many situations where it came down to pinning an inmate to the floor and injecting him with a strong tranquilizer rather than risking him assaulting someone or killing himself. When the incident is over and they have calmed down, we resume teaching them about the triggers, side effects, and course of their illness. We encourage them to work with Health Services by taking their medications. Psychological counseling serves as an adjunct to medication but not a substitute. Once stabilized, we can try to treat their illness using the "talking cure."

There are many cases where violent criminal histories can be directly attributed to mental illness even though the individual did a great job of masking it. Unlike the mentally ill in the free world clinics, these men have the street smarts to conceal their pathology. Once on medication, they look much better. We had incarcerated a schizophrenic man who stalked a woman to her church and burned it down in a rage of longing after she entered it. (Fortunately, she got out in time.) Now that he is incarcerated and on medication, he is a peaceful, pleasant individual who wouldn't hurt a soul. We had a U.S. Veteran who attacked a family during a parade when he psychotically mistook them for enemy soldiers from his Vietnam experience. (Fortunately, no one was hurt in this incident either.) We had a psychotic man incarcerated for violently attacking a police officer for a minor provocation. Now he openly defends the authority of officers in the prison and is embarrassed by his past behavior. Another psychotic man robbed a bank during a manic episode but was so disorganized he couldn't find his way out of the bank and got caught wandering around the basement of the bank looking for an exit. On medication, he is astute and organized. Although incarceration facilitates medication compliance and guarantees regular therapy visits, one supposes there are better means to manage the mentally ill.

We have also had several men who arrived here without a diagnosed mental illness but were found to be severely psychotic when under the closer scrutiny of prison. Officer observations, the stress of incarceration, or the latent emergence of psychosis yielded evidence of schizophrenia the inmate attempted to hide. Colorful language sometimes gives them away. The Warden sent me a letter from an inmate convinced that his arrest was a government conspiracy to prevent him from revealing state secrets. He complained that he was "stuck in Big Sister's vagina." An investigation revealed a man who had become completely psychotic and needed compassionate treatment for paranoia. In such severe cases where inmates are actively psychotic, we transfer them to prison psychiatric facilities where they may spend the remainder of their incarceration.

The stressed out

During their first incarceration, many men experience some level of stress but it's within what we consider "normal limits." Prison is a tense environment. For inmates new to the system, feeling "stressed" is probably a normal reaction that could mobilize their energies to address significant challenges.

It might be their needed wake-up call. The best stress preventative is probably dealing with the issue through constructive activity and focus. Responding to family problems, finding work, staying out of trouble, developing a plan for living in prison, and avoiding conflict all ameliorate the tensions. Of course, if the individual is continually feeling overwhelmed, irritable, and symptomatic it's time for more intensive counseling and medication.

The depressed

Another common problem here is sadness. As with stress, we don't encourage them to run from it. Sadness, too, is a healthy human response, this time due to significant loss. Many men have lost every meaningful relationship they had on the outside. They may fear expressing despondency because it can be associated with weakness and dependency. Men hate to appear vulnerable and naturally build walls around their pain. Inmates, however, will experience and therefore must grieve many losses due to incarceration. We don't want to interfere with that grieving process because it eventually can result in a person becoming emotionally stronger. It might help them mobilize for making needed personality changes.

When men come to us complaining of significant depression we generally advise them to "go through the motions" of a normal day, even if they aren't feeling any connection to those activities. After exploring their experiences of guilt, loneliness, and sadness, we also ask them to look at other incarcerated people who have created meaning despite incarceration. Eventually, they will emerge with a sense of possibilities for their future. Finding new interests within the prison gates is a good indicator that the individual has started to turn the corner.

The traumatized

Perhaps the most under-reported diagnoses in the prisons are the Post Traumatic Stress Disorders (PTSD). Some men develop PTSD having been sexually assaulted in prison but far more come to prison with PTSD after participating in violence in their own communities. Many young men joined gangs with no idea how gruesomely bloody they could be. Now they have nightmares, flashbacks, and a psychological numbing because of over-exposure to horrific scenes. Some are too embarrassed to report the trauma for fear of looking weak. Others are worried they will get in legal trouble if they come forward. They keep quiet and suffer in silence, relying on medication to calm their nerves. They might lose sleep and have intrusive thoughts during the day. They might have moments of panic or present as emotionally numb. They don't feel whole but are frightened to tell anyone why.

Incarcerated war veterans also suffer from PTSD and are also ambivalent about seeking help in prison. They attribute their drug abuse, mental illness, and criminal behaviors to their tours of duty and combat stress, whether it was in Vietnam, Iraq, or Afghanistan. They complain that rather than receive help for their problems they were incarcerated by the government that had promised to stand by them. Feeling they deserved better from Uncle Sam, they alternately feel shame at how far they've fallen and pride about the service they provided their country.

The anxious

Men who become anxious about germs, closed places, and being in crowded areas naturally have trouble adjusting to prison. There are many slobbery, dirty inmates here so everyone is exposed to germs while there never seems to be enough disinfectant. There are many tight, confined places people can get locked in, increasing their anxieties about infection and contamination. Tight confinement also tends to induce panic attacks for those constitutionally inclined. Remarkably, many phobias resolve in prison. Perhaps they are receiving the treatment of choice for phobias, "flooding," which involves a high level of exposure to the anxiety producing event. Although we don't apply it scientifically, it appears to reduce during incarceration.

The sleepless

Many inmates report sleep disturbance and for many reasons. There is the change in their routine, activity level, and diet; worries about family, new charges, and assaults; distractions via noise levels, card games, and snoring; a thin mattress and a creaking cot; cell mates with different shifts; officers putting a flashlight in their face during count; withdrawal from drugs and alcohol; and guilt feelings for past lawlessness and ruined lives. After several days without sleep there is a marked deterioration in presentation and functioning. Men stagger into our offices with puffy eyes, looking miserable, asking for help. They complain of discomfort, emotionality, and memory problems. Some even become disoriented and psychotic. People need sleep to function.

Fortunately, the symptoms resolve when the person gets sufficient rest.

Generally we recommend "sleep hygiene" practices that are also used on the outside such as staying awake during the daytime, exercising to tire the body, buying ear plugs to reduce noise levels, and avoiding caffeine after lunch. We avoid prescribing medication because sleeping pills are addictive. Also, drug- seeking inmates would routinely complain of sleep deprivation if they knew it would get them tranquilizers. As with phobias remitting, eventually most men learn to fall asleep because their bodies force them to.

The angry

Anger is a constant problem. Some is due to the pressure cooker environment of a prison but generally these men brought anger problems with them to prison. For many, it was the cause of their incarceration. Men tend to use anger as a primary emotion for when things go wrong. It's the default emotion. You're feeling insignificant? Fight someone. You're feeling trapped? Break something. Experiencing loneliness? Lash out. Many men feel more comfortable experiencing anger rather than emotions that suggest vulnerability. Part of the job then is to address the actual issue rather than pacifying the "angry" experience. The best place to address such anger problems is in a group setting where men benefit from listening to the experiences of others as well as participating.

In some instances, an inmate's anger is a normal emotional experience in response to having been wronged or experiencing an injustice. In such cases, the anger can be used constructively. The goal of treatment is not always to prevent people from getting angry. However, angry displays will usually get a person hurt in prison and needs to be contained. That's why our first step in counseling is to encourage them to take a step back, avoid overreacting, consult with us about the source of their anger, and think carefully about handling their situation.

The explosive

In addition to men with more typical anger problems, there are usually men in every prison who have problems with "emotional regulation." Interpersonal hurts and insults that most of us would ignore can completely unhinge them. Technically their diagnoses are not in the "severe psychopathology" range but they are still major management problems and are time-intensive cases for psychologists. These inmates also demonstrate shifts in self-esteem and self-harming behaviors like cutting on themselves and head banging. Once other inmates learn about their strange behaviors, they tend to be avoided which only exacerbates the problem. We had to develop a whole unit for them in one of our prisons to provide a secure, stabilizing environment with sufficient staffing.

The suicidal

Every man will have his breaking point. I know of several men who committed suicide prior to trial and each for a different reason. One man couldn't handle the withdrawal symptoms from heroin. A medical doctor couldn't face the disapproval of his young family after he was arrested in a sex sting operation. He was planning to visit the home of a little girl after believing he got the mother's permission via internet to have sex with her. He didn't know he was talking to a federal agent. A white collar criminal was being squeezed by the FBI to accept more years in prison under a plea agreement to help his family avoid getting charged in his conspiracy. Not being able to see any acceptable way out, he committed suicide under the pressure. Another inmate made bogus allegations against staff members in his suicide note, thinking it would strengthen his family's million dollar lawsuit against the government. In essence, his suicide was part apology to his family for what he had done and part money-making scheme to compensate them for the troubles he had caused. Unfortunately, the accused staff had to tolerate a lengthy, stressful investigation.

While some men suicide due to mental illness, more often it is caused by factors such as the pressures of prison life, individual personality problems, and an inability to identify credible solutions. One inmate who lived by the convict code decided that he couldn't deal with his shame and the harassment he would receive from owing money to several gangs who he couldn't pay back. He had no family to bail him out and no friends to loan him money, so he tried to kill himself. Another inmate had been incarcerated for years but used weekly contact from his family and frequent phone calls home to sustain him. He had never been in "the hole" before so he was not accustomed to doing time without his family's support. As correctional officers would say, he had been "living on the street," never really learning to adjust to prison. When he got caught violating a rule and placed in a segregated housing unit, he became so overwhelmed and depressed by the isolation from family that he attempted suicide.

As there are many reasons for suicide, there are many methods. The most common method for men on the street is a gunshot to the head but it's not so easy in prison. Here, most men hang themselves. When you see them, their head and upper torso are suspended just a few feet from the floor with a tourniquet around their neck tied to the metal frame of their bed. Other men use tourniquets to cut off the blood supply to their head until they lapse into a coma and die while lying in their bed. Men also cut their wrists or necks but it is sometimes hard to get a sharpened tool and the blood is too easily noticed by passers by. Men who have tried and failed told me that the bones and ligaments of the wrists and neck made it difficult to cut the right arteries. Further, they say the cutting itself is extremely painful which dissuaded them from trying it a second time.

Pills used to be a preferred method but this agency now administers pills in crushed form so inmates can't cheek them to accumulate a lethal dose. Inmates have tried jumping off high floors but it potentially results in brain damage and paralysis but not death, quite painful and then impossible to commit suicide the next time. A young man almost bled himself to death with a thousand nicks from a piece of tin foil he got off an air freshener that a staff member had left behind. He placed a shower curtain under his mattress to catch all the blood so passing guards wouldn't notice a pool of blood on the floor. Fortunately, an astute guard noticed his pallid complexion.

We have learned from bitter experience that suicidal people can even attempt suicide while on constant observation in a suicide watch room. A person wedged his head inside a toilet bowl to die by drowning. A man hid the plastic from the packaged food provided, then tied those pieces together to make a tourniquet with which to hang himself. A man pulled the stitching from his mattress to attempt to hang himself. Men have tried to electrocute themselves with the light socket. Someone intentionally choked himself by swallowing a wad of torn out pages from a bible that a gullible officer provided him. An inmate jumped off his bed and tried to land directly on his head to snap his neck. A man cut off his blood supply by fashioning gauze bandages into a tourniquet around his neck while pretending to sleep under a blanket. We can't assume that once someone is placed on watch they will be safe. That's why when we examine a suicide watch room we try to imagine every feature inside as a possible means to suicide. Inmates sometimes accuse us of cruelly withholding their property when they are placed on watch. We withhold because we learned that determined men can be ingenious in devising methods to end their lives.

Although men try to "end it all" in prison, on a per capita basis there are fewer suicides in our prison than in the free world. Over the past 10 years there have been fewer than 10 suicides per 100,000 people[4] in the federal prison whereas in the free world the suicide rate for men has been about 18 per 100,000. This is surprising given the stress of prison and the fact that it is not a naturally hopeful place. Should we consider it a testament to an effective system? Probably our success is best attributed to the fact that officers are trained to be alert to signs of depression and that psychologists are responsive to officer referrals. Remarkably, even inmates are encouraged to refer inmates who appear depressed or suicidal. While they are uncomfortable about "snitching", they do it anyway because they don't want to be responsible for a death. Generally, though, they request that their referral stay confidential. (The exception to inmates alerting staff is when they happen upon a completed suicide. In that case, they might not report it for fear that they will be suspected of murder.)

Psychologists believe that the main cause of suicide is depression, but in my experience it is not exactly the depression that drives the suicide. It's the sense of demoralization that follows the depression. In other words, depressed individuals start imagining that they will never feel better so they decide to "end the pain". We constantly explain to them that suicide is "a permanent solution to a temporary problem." Many inmates were sure they had nothing to live for but then discovered those reasons through counseling. Hope is often the best antidote.

A 40 year-old man who never married or had children due to being incarcerated throughout adulthood had become suicidal. He couldn't conceive of a reason to stay alive, especially because people on the outside had gradually stopped visiting and he became convinced no one cared. He still had plenty of time to do and his prospects did indeed look bleak. At first I struggled just as he did with identifying what could make his life meaningful for him because none of the normal anchors that inmates depend on seemed to be working. However, he remembered that the niece and nephew of his divorced sister looked up to him and might even need him. After some positive letter exchanges with them, he resolved to become successful as a person and in prison in order to support them and make their lives better. That was his healthy turnaround that made his incarceration bearable.

The assaulted

While we closely monitor and treat those who have been sexually assaulted, our primary goal is preventing sexual abuse. Towards this goal we practice a "zero tolerance" policy for sexual assaults. To my knowledge, not a single verified case of a reported rape has occurred at this low security prison. Several inmates have reported to me that they were sexually assaulted and raped at other prisons but not here. I have also had inmates tell me that in the County Jails they have been sexually assaulted but even that has been improving over the years. Recent legislation has focused jail administrations on the seriousness of sexual assaults in prison. White inmates will report being sexually assaulted when placed in large holding tanks with a majority black inmate population. Statistics back up their claim. I have not heard of similar problems for black or Hispanic inmates but that doesn't mean it doesn't occur. Men who have been sexually assaulted are mentally "off," often damaged, either with diagnosable conditions like schizophrenia and psychotic disorder, or more likely with a generalized traumatic reaction resulting in poor sleep, startle responses, anxiety, depression, low self-esteem, and frequent preoccupation and fear.

Many men report having come close to being assaulted at this prison and it is certainly possible that there have been unreported assaults. Oftentimes, male victims won't report perpetrators even in cases of sexual assault. It's another reason why officers have to be active and vigilant in finding out what's going on in the housing units. Some men have reported to me during psychology sessions that they were extorted, threatened, pushed, manhandled, manipulated, and bribed to perform oral sex but in their telling they refused or escaped. Whenever there is an allegation of a sexual assault the individuals are separated and a full investigation is launched. If there is sufficient evidence, the alleged predator is prosecuted. At the very least, he is shipped to another institution with clear documentation labeling his propensities. I had a man describe "the most frightening night of his life" occurring at 2:00 am when an inmate tried to sexually assault him in a dark hallway on his way to the bathroom. He spent the rest of the evening with his boots and clothes on, fully awake, holding onto the bed frame of his bed, too terrorized to return to sleep or walk down the other hallway to report the incident. He waited hours for morning to come so he could report what occurred in the relative safety of the morning light.

I've also had my fair share of false alarms. One New Year's Eve I was called into the local hospital at 1:00 in the morning on a possible sexual assault. An officer making rounds in his housing unit found an inmate lying face down in the bathroom, underwear pulled below his knees, blood streaming from his behind, and he was out cold. Very reasonably the assumption was an assault had taken place and he was rushed to the hospital. I spoke to the Emergency Room Medical Doctor immediately afterwards and he explained to me, "He has polyps on his intestines. They burst when he was on the toilet which released lots of blood. He became light headed, fell forward hitting his head against the bathroom stall door, and then fell to the floor where he was knocked unconscious." There was no sexual assault but for reassurance I questioned the doctor again and he told me, "Look, I appreciate you guys being concerned about sexual assaults in prison, but this guy just had a burst polyp, that's it." Then he walked away from me seemingly irritated that I had taken up his time on this busy shift.

The addicted

Drug abuse is probably the most common pre-incarceration "mental health" problem that inmates experienced. Depending on the survey, 40% to 60% of inmates report having abused drugs prior to prison.[5] Most are not interested in receiving treatment. About one quarter of the drug abusers, or about 15% of the inmate population, will volunteer for the program. By law it is voluntary so prison authorities will encourage inmates but cannot force them to participate. It's unfortunate more don't want treatment since the link between drug-taking and crime is indisputable, even though the pathways often vary.

Oftentimes, criminality leads to drug abuse. Drug abusing for some is a recreational activity. They lived on the fringes and took drugs as part of their antisocial, party lifestyles. Other inmates report how drug abuse preceded their criminality. For them, drugs were the gateway to crime rather than its traveling companion. The story repeats itself in interview after interview. The men describe feeling lost, bored, having marital conflicts, financial worries and dead end jobs. They are looking to relieve feelings of being aimless, eventually gravitating towards people in similar circumstances. Drugs provide fun and relief from the hopelessness. The individual then embarks on a downward spiral of irresponsibility. Eventually they fully enter the world of criminality, selling drugs and manufacturing them, in an effort to maintain their costly habit. Inevitably they get caught. Then in prison they go through detoxification and drug treatment, and finally mourn the life they lost. As it has been said, "Whiskey man does the crime, but straight man does the time." The use of intensive treatment programs in prisons have been essential in helping these men first manage their cravings and then find better ways of living their lives.

The sex offenders

Sex offenders are the fastest growing prison population in the federal system. In the 1990s, approximately 1% of our inmate population had current convictions for sex offenses. By 2010, that number had increased to 5% of the inmate population having current convictions for sex offenses.[6] Of those, at the low security prison almost all of them are for child pornography. More perhaps than any other population in the prison, viewers of child pornography experience a drastic negative change in their lives once arrested. Many were pillars of the community: attorneys, medical doctors, and business professionals. Often they were family men raising apparently healthy, loving families. In their minds, they were 95% good people but had this dirty, dark secret that occupied just 5% of their lives- one surreptitious bad habit of perusing child pornography on the computer late at night in their studies. Who would know or care? Their family was asleep and they were in the privacy of their homes. Then someone with whom they swapped child photographs gets busted and brings down the whole network of men involved in trading pictures on the internet. Because it was the "world wide web," the pictures technically crossed state lines which violates interstate transport laws and makes it a federal offense.

Not all men go no further than viewing child pornography. Some men eventually go on to trying to satisfy their aberrant desires by arranging a sexual liaison. Some go to online chat rooms in order to entice a child or young teen into meeting with them. What they didn't know was that the person they were communicating with was an undercover FBI agent. They themselves are eventually lured to a public location thinking they are going to have a sexual rendezvous but instead get arrested. Carrying gifts for children, lubricants, alcohol, and condoms, they have no credible excuse. They get "outed" to the world when the story hits the newspapers and eventually get incarcerated. Of course, their life can never be the same.

When they arrive in prison, guards might treat them as just any other inmate which is enough of a perceived degradation. But it gets worse because in inmate society they are on the bottom rung. Further, depending on how public their crime was they may have to stay locked down in a single cell for their own protection. Their families often reject them as well. Unlike criminals whose families might have known about their illegal activities and perhaps even benefited from them, sex offender families feel utterly betrayed, shamed, and confused. The man they thought they knew is not the pedophile they are learning about. This is sufficient cause for rejection. The spouse is also concerned that child protective agencies might consider her complicit, which makes her vulnerable to prosecution and the children's removal from the home. In disgust, self-interest, and with the urging of others, the spouse might completely abandon the offender. In the immediate aftermath, some men contemplate suicide. Then, surprisingly, after the initial depressive period many adjust, come to terms with the loss of their families, and make the necessary social accommodations to prison. Those with self-absorbed personalities have fewer difficulties starting anew.

Some pedophiles are family men with a deep dark secret but many are single men, sex addicts who spent uninterrupted hours viewing a range of pornography. When the agents bust in the door, these guys might be unshaven, sitting in their underwear, eyes glued to the computer screen, with a bottle of urine on the desk because they were too engrossed to walk away from the computer screen. Our experience has been that some men were sex voyeurs rather than pedophiles, having thousands of pornographic images only some of which involved children. It doesn't change the fact that those photographed were being victimized. In any case, even if the collections have only a few images of children, it is sufficient to prosecute them if the intent to possess them can be proven. Understandably, society is concerned about these men being out in the free world before they have served their time and also made substantial personal and psychological changes. No one with a family wants potential perpetrators living next door. In response, the federal prisons have developed excellent treatment programs for sex offenders. These inmates, like drug abusers, get as much as a full year of intensive group therapy treatments when they volunteer to participate. Although they can refuse to participate in prison treatment, they may be required to participate in treatment after releasing as a condition of their probation.

Chapter 3

Medical, Legal, and Family Issues

"I fought the law and the law won."
Bobby Fuller Four lyrics

Medical Issues

Due to longer sentences, improved healthcare, and an aging criminal population, there has been a significant increase in the resources spent caring for the elderly in prison. Although there are policies that permit compassionate release from prison, it is usually reserved for people within a few months of dying and in practice it is rarely approved. I'm told the agency once released a man due to cancer but that he fully recovered from his illness and lived a long life without serving out his sentence. The public resents such miscarriages of justice. So gradually the agency has tightened requirements. Now inmates get transferred to medical institutions to finish their terms.

The senile are at risk for assault if not transferred to the appropriate medical facility. At this institution we've had several inmates become senile during their incarceration. We had an elderly man take another man's underwear when leaving the showers that caused quite a ruckus. Another senile inmate got confused late one night, walked into the wrong cell, and crawled into another man's bed. Fortunately, the man didn't over-react and the confusion was resolved without incident. We had a confused elderly man wander into the wrong workplace and spend half the day cleaning before it was noticed. An elderly inmate who lost all of his inhibitions with his medical condition made derogatory comments about a young hothead's wife. Fortunately, several inmates intervened to calm the situation and nothing bad came of it. Once staff members have identified these men, we try to find them the appropriate medication and send them to facilities that provide appropriate care. Thuggish inmates, anxious to prove themselves, might mistake senility for disrespect and use it as a pretext to fight.

Men also come to Psychology with a range of somatic complaints for which the medical doctors were unable to find medical causes. These men neither have medical conditions, nor are they malingering. Their mental health problems are being channeled into medical concerns and emerge as somatic delusions. We had a man stop eating because his "stomach was broken;" a man convinced for years he was dying of heart failure despite numerous tests confirming his good health; a man who could feel that his "spine needed screws because it was falling apart;" and, a man convinced that an animal had entered his rectum because he could feel the scratching. These delusions are very hard to treat. If they persist in demanding medical treatment, delusional men such as these can't make it at a standard prison and eventually get sent to psychiatric facilities for treatment and to serve out their time.

I've met several inmates who struggled with a terminal illness in prison. Prison is not a good place to die. There was a man dying of AIDS who was becoming more and more emotional due to his illness. We do not have sophisticated ways of dealing with men who rant and rave. The average prison has few options- freedom within the gates or getting locked up. Within a prison setting there are not various levels of care. In this particular case, we could not transfer the man to a medical facility because he was waiting for the court to take up his immigration issue. Towards the end, as we would pass by and see him lying in bed too weak to raise his head, he would wave at us to keep going as we made our rounds. He told me that he hoped to be convicted so he could move on to a medical facility to get the care he needed. The Warden got involved and he eventually got his court hearing. As he had hoped, he was found guilty of immigration violations and sentenced to three years of incarceration. He was on his way to a medical facility the next morning, thankful for the turn of events. As he put it, if he had contracted AIDs in his home country, he would be a dead man.

Most inmates are not sympathetic to the problems of overwhelmed prison medical professionals who are constantly besieged with medical complaints. Ironically, the most understanding patient I met here was a medical doctor himself. He was dying with colon cancer that had gone undiagnosed until its later stages. When I met with him I assumed he would rail against the care he had received and the late diagnosis. Instead, he explained to me that tests don't always pick up cancers, the procedures used by this facility were standard medical care, that his type of cancer typically evades detection, and that there was no one to blame. Shortly thereafter he transferred to a prison hospital to get the surgery that might save him. In this case, medical knowledge inoculated him from blaming medical staff for his disease.

Legal issues

Conspiracy laws were designed to prosecute participants in organized criminal enterprises but criminal groups working in the most loosely coordinated fashion can be prosecuted under these laws. The ring leader, who is well represented legally, is smart enough to set up a subordinate as the fall guy. I have seen simple men of low intelligence, who described themselves as gofers, get prosecuted as the "Syndicate Leader" and get more time than anyone in his group. Throughout the trial, they may be unaware that all of their co-defendants have already begun cooperating with the government while they are being encouraged by "friends" to keep quiet. Once convicted, and they learn that they got more time than co-conspirators, they realize the injustice. When they tell the prison psychologists what happened, we can only refer them back to their attorneys.

Given the conspiracy laws, set-ups, conflicts, and monitoring, you can understand why paranoia is common. It generally takes time for psychologists to sort out what is normal, healthy fear and what is evidence of mental illness. An inmate whose rape conviction was discovered by other inmates reported that his machine at the factory had been sabotaged, that he hears his name being spoken in whispered tones, and that he kept having the same inmate sitting near him listening in on his conversations. He started staying in his boots and trying to remain alert most nights to prevent an assault. Was he being set up or just irrationally worried? Only time would tell. When I reported my concerns to an evening officer, he had an unusual take on the situation: "Man, he must have it good. He thinks everyone cares about him." We followed procedure and locked him up for his own safety, which satisfied him while we investigated his concerns and gave him an opportunity to catch up on his sleep. The result of our investigation was that it was "psychological" and that there was no one "out to get him."

The older inmates with long sentences have their own "club" at this low. Compared to the younger men they might seem bitterer about their incarceration. Many have done time in tougher joints. They are forced to see other men come and go. A prison refrain I once heard was "got five- keep it alive, got ten- start again, but twenty? Man, that's plenty." As it was explained to me, inmates with less time can maintain their families, those with more time can start new ones, but those who have very long sentences must focus on creating a productive life inside the gates because they'll have no one out there when they release. These men tend to find meaning within the gates by creating a smaller uninterrupted existence. Young inmates who try to challenge these experienced convicts because they look so reserved will be surprised by how tough they really are.

Some men are never able to settle into being in a jail or to accepting their sentences. They spend their energies trying to reverse their conviction or reduce their sentence. No matter how guilty, how debt-ridden their families, how reliant on wishful thinking, they depend on the appeal process to get them out early. It's as much a psychological maneuver as a legal one. I once told an inmate whose case seemed particularly far-fetched that only 1% win on appeal and he said, "Yeah, and I'm that 1%." One inmate had a double life sentence which he took to court. He reduced the first life sentence to 20 years and is back in court now trying to appeal the more difficult second sentence. He acknowledges that the first appeal was the stronger one. Although understandable, it is also sad that he is devoting so much energy to what even he acknowledges is a lost cause. A bad police officer who was just convicted on drug charges and involvement in several witnessed burglaries is cheerful in all my interactions with him. He swears that he is innocent and will beat it on appeal. I wished him luck because at this early stage of incarceration even false hope is better than absolute despair. Several inmates I see regularly at the jail each received more than two hundred years for their convictions but are also already planning their appeals. Their lawyers explained that some of the sentencing laws over using firearms during the commission of crimes are being overturned. They are hopeful that it will significantly reduce their sentences. But even if that were the case, I don't imagine they will be able to leave prison alive given the length of their sentences. Still, they stay hopeful.

Inmates seize on every rumor that they might get released early through legislative action. When the government gets into debt, they think prisoners will be freed to save money; when the government goes to war, they believe there will be a draft option for felons to keep "the good boys" out of war; and when the administration changes political parties, they hope for clemency for certain categories of offenses. Although these hopes are inevitably dashed, the rumor mill provides excitement. I monitored an inmate's phone call where he explained to his wife that a federal parole system might be implemented to honor a Congresswoman active in prison legislation since she had just died. His wife laughed at him on the phone and said, "You guys just live on hope. You think Americans will let a bunch of criminals out early cause some old lady died?" and with those comments burst his balloon. Inmates come to consult with me all the time on the latest rumors. I used to try to provide them matter of fact information but the negative implications seemed to upset them. Now, realizing they are clinging to pipe dreams to ward off depression and pass the time, I am vague and say something like, "We will just have to see how that one turns out." One legal change did result in inmates leaving early. There was a reduction in sentences for dealers who distributed crack vs. powder cocaine to end the disparities in sentences between these two groups. Men serving twenty years were suddenly out the door in ten. In that instance, there was less rumor and inmates left quietly for fear that too much talk would squelch it.

Inmates don't brag as they approach their release date. Other inmates might place contraband on them to sabotage their plans. Misery loves company and no one is more miserable than inmates with long sentences. I tell new inmates with short sentences to stop complaining for that reason. They don't always listen. I saw several men serve out the last few months of their incarceration in lock-down status because they were being threatened. They are easy marks for assaults and extortion because they can't afford to act out for fear of losing earned good time. I know of one case where an inmate tried to force another inmate into a sexual relationship by threatening to ruin his release plans should he resist. Of course, inmates with extensive gambling debts will seek protection by getting locked up towards the end of their sentence in an effort to avoid paying creditors. Among prison buddies, though, release is bittersweet. Sometimes there are quiet going away parties for inmates the night before release. Since they are not permitted contact with each other afterwards, these goodbyes are generally final.

Possible injustice: Rarely does one knowingly come across innocence in this system but instances of injustice occur. For example, non- U.S. citizens are deported to their country of origin after serving their federal time if involved in drug convictions. Fair enough, since these individuals violated our laws. But what about young men who were smuggled into the U.S. as infants and have never lived in another country? Some of these men have their whole family living here as citizens, have married and raised children here but never obtained U.S. citizenship. Some don't even speak another language. Convicted of a drug offense, they will serve several years in a federal prison and after completing their sentence will get deported. Essentially they will lose contact with their children, wives, and families, while also having to start over in a foreign country, possibly one in which they don't speak the language. Wives might file for divorce early on and tell the children they won't see their father again. That is a tough road to hoe for a first conviction.

Imprisoned men often complain that the system is rigged against them. If they take their case to trial rather than plead guilty, they might receive four times the sentence. An offense that may have warranted a 5-year incarceration in a plea deal becomes a 20-year offense if taken to trial. Even the innocent would hesitate to contest charges under those circumstances. Defense attorneys often urge defendants to accept a guilty plea for precisely this reason. One inmate who had been charged with drug dealing had his money confiscated by the police as part of what he perceived to be an illegal search and seizure. By his account this left him too broke to get adequate representation. He reports that as a result he was forced to use a disinterested public defender (in his particular case) while facing a skilled prosecutor who happened to have been mentored by his presiding judge. He lamented, "It's a dirty card game with everyone allowed to cheat but the defendant."

Once a person is incarcerated, the administration of justice changes. If something prohibited or illegal happens near an inmate, he is presumed to be involved and will be locked up while investigators try to obtain information. If his cell mate hides contraband like drugs or weapons in the cell he will certainly get locked up. If near an assault, he will probably get rounded up and investigated. Beating a charge in prison is difficult because the system has to rely on secret finger pointing to reduce the risk of retribution against witnesses. I have seen inmates insist they were innocent but other inmates confidentially identified them as the culprit so they were found guilty. Similarly, I have seen many situations in which inmates who were rounded up had witnessed, but didn't participate in, wrong-doing. They are left with the difficult choice of "snitching" and risking retaliation if found out or keeping their mouths closed and possibly getting sanctioned. There are no easy answers. While I help them problem solve their dilemma in my role as a psychologist and privately confer with investigating officials, I don't pretend to offer them a "solution." My own view is that they should risk getting "found out" by telling investigators what they know but I don't live in the prisons so it's easy for me to say.

Inmates have been fired from their jobs because they were with an unproductive work crew even though they had tried their personal best. Inmates have been sanctioned for fighting when they were essentially trying to protect themselves during an assault but possibly went over the line by pushing back. When inmates have bad experiences such as this they personalize it and imagine they are being set up. When they come to me with this type of paranoia, I sometimes try to explain the bureaucracy to them but they argue that it must be intentional because "no organization can be that dumb." What they don't realize is that by strictly sanctioning inmates for associating with trouble we make inmates alert to avoiding even the appearance of wrongdoing, which ultimately serves the orderly running of the institution. That's why an inmate who learns his cell mate is involved in something illegal should request a cell change. It is a way of avoiding trouble before it happens. Inmates who are repeatedly turned down can at least argue, "I was trying to get away but you guys wouldn't get the message". Of course, if they gave us specific information that their cellmate was "dirty," they wouldn't have to worry about getting sanctioned. Smart inmates who are aware of wrong-doing will do what they can to avoid those locations and disassociate themselves from inmates they know to be trouble makers.

All inmates start out by saying they are innocent. When I first started running therapy groups, I would start each group by having inmates go around and discuss their criminal history. They would all start the same way, "They say I committed (fill in the blank) but I was innocent of the charges." It started off each group with a big, fat lie and made a mockery of the principles of therapy so finally I gave up on that exercise. Since then I've learned that most inmates will eventually confide they engaged knowingly in some kind of criminal activity. Due to poor legal representation, unfortunate politics, overzealous prosecutors, or an ornery judge, many men believe they got excessively long sentences but very few complain, at least in private, that they were innocent of the charges and hadn't committed a crime.

I've met thousands of inmates and I suppose almost all of them were guilty in one way or another with very few exceptions. One exception was an elderly medical doctor who told me he was unaware of the fraud perpetrated in his name. I believe him. He was a retiring doctor who agreed to work ten hours per week for a small local practice to provide a bit of extra retirement money. Devoted to his patients and perhaps not as sharp as he used to be, he was insufficiently discerning when he signed paperwork as his business administrator directed him to do. As it turned out, the billing was excessive and he was charged with fraud. As his lawyer had advised him, he pled guilty because if he took it to trial he risked a much longer sentence. His lawyer explained that at a trial the prosecutor would have him sit next to all his guilty co-conspirators, making it very difficult to convince jurors that he was an unwitting dupe. In his case, protesting his innocence would be tantamount to doubling the length of his incarceration. Because he didn't want to risk abandoning his wife, children, and especially his grandchildren for longer than he had to, he took the plea bargain. I reviewed his paperwork and see no reason to question this story.

Another case where I was convinced the individual was innocent was a Mexican man who says he was used as a drug mule. By his report, he grew up in an impoverished Mexican town with a collectivist culture where people depend on each other for favors. An elderly neighbor lent his car to this man so he could pick up a sick relative in the United States. He was not aware that drugs had been hidden in his vehicle and they were found during the border inspection. He was given a sentence of 3 years. He seemed genuine in his shock of having been used as a courier and cursed bitterly about the betrayal. Of course, there is no way of knowing what he knew when crossing the border. Apparently, the evidence was clear in court that he was transporting drugs and so now he is an incarcerated felon.

When one hears about prosecutorial errors through Barry Scheck's Innocence Project, or misconduct in high profile cases such as the 2006 Duke University rape accusation case and the 2009 conviction of Alaska's Senator Stevens, one wonders if the average Joe can get a fair shake. Perhaps it's not surprising when the poor get less than sufficient representation. But if wealthy individuals, who hire the best lawyers and have the megaphone of a national press corps can barely get their story heard, what chance is there for the rest of us?

Family Issues

Institutions support direct family communication through visitation, telephone contact, and letters, despite it requiring a significant investment in staff time. It's of tremendous benefit overall. It improves morale, provides a "window to the world," and keeps them current which will help them adjust to reentry. Family visiting occurs in a large room. Policy allows a hug and kiss between inmates and their families when they first see each other, hand-holding throughout the visit, and hugging and kissing again when they say good bye. Visiting hours are generous so families who want to see an inmate on even a weekly basis can do so. Telephone privileges are even more user-friendly. Mail comes by the bucketful and indigent inmates get free stamps until they earn their first paycheck. Recently, institutions have implemented an e-mail system so inmates can write family and receive emails in real time, which has become extremely popular.

Despite this accessibility, there are problems for inmates maintaining family contact. For example, because the agency is federal, inmates might be moved hundred of miles away from their families due to population issues in the prison. When a Mexican inmate found out he was transferring even further from the border, effectively hampering family contact, he poignantly asked, "Illegal aliens don't get visits from their family?" and I admit staff was rather discomfited by the question. Furthermore, there are long lines for visiting: prisons are often in remote, rural areas; visiting facilities are inadequate because they were built long ago for a much smaller inmate population and there aren't funds to enlarge them; and some family members resent going through metal detectors (for weapons), ion scanners (for drugs), and pat searches (for contraband, generally). So while the agency has a fairly liberal degree of visitation, mail, and telephone communication there are still obstacles. More importantly, families often don't want contact with inmates and find excuses for not coming. By their own admission, many of these men were bad husbands and fathers and so prison is a great opportunity for families to say goodbye, guilt-free and safely.

One inmate described his drug abuse and criminal activity as "an emotional tsunami" that drove away everyone except his 12 year old son who was "incredibly rooted" to him. Family members remember the drugs, physical abuse, stealing, absences, and chaos, and look forward to building a life without the drain of a drug-addicted, domineering criminal to worry about. Two children who had been victims of their father's sexual abuse surprised staff when they indicated they would like to visit him in the hospital while he was on life support following his heart attack. They used some of the time to confront him about his past. When he finally lapsed into a coma, they quickly decided to withdraw life support explaining they were anxious not to miss their flight home. In our drug program, there is an exercise in which family members write letters to the inmates about what their lives were like prior to his incarceration. Those stories, read aloud by inmates to the group, regularly elicit inmate crying because they are confronted with all the hardship, pain, and soul-killing experiences that their loved ones had to endure because of them.

Inmates sometimes ask families not to visit because they feel humiliated, don't want to be inconvenienced, have girlfriends and competing families, or hate having to go through strip searches on their way into and out of the visiting room. Many inmates report that having to say goodbye to their children at the end of the visitation is so painful that they prefer not to have the visit in the first place. Other inmates report that it is hard to "do their time" worrying about family so they prefer to cut off contact when they walk in the gates. Of course, as is typical with such men, they don't consider what is best for their families. Since men tend to prefer to solve problems through action rather than emotional support, they feel impotent when family members come in to the visiting room and report on all the family problems that are going on that they can't help resolve.

When inmates learn that their wives want a divorce, there is usually a lot of begging, demanding, and manipulating by the inmates, followed by a visit to the Psychology Department for support. It is our job to talk with the inmate about his rage, sense of betrayal, loss, and emotional pain. Since it occurs often enough, there are also many fellow inmates who provide consolation. Of course, the hardened criminals who learn of another inmate's divorce take this as an opportunity to pour salt in the wounds or laugh and mimic his distress. "Yeah, she's probably screwing the boss right now," one man told his distraught cellmate. When wives divorce, children often divorce as well. Courts won't insist that ex-wives take their children to a prison to meet with the father. Grandparents oftentimes don't have the authority to do so. When wives leave them, inmates are doubly hurt to learn they will lose contact with their children as well. Phone calls home get declined, letters go unanswered, and they find how tenuous a child's expressions of love are and how dependent on the supervising parent. We try to console them about the possibilities of re-connecting with their kids upon release but it's an admittedly weak substitute.

Men who receive "Dear John" letters are fortunate that at least their wives are taking the time to thoughtfully explain their reasons and usually do so with some compassion. More typical is when guys call home and never seem to catch their wives in. Then one day another man answers the phone. Inmates jokingly refer to this as "finding out about Sancho." In several instances I've received calls from the ex-spouse who wants me as a Psychologist to tell her husband that she is leaving him. For reasons of confidentiality and to avoid creating "dual relationships," I can't counsel her nor relay her messages to him. Female officers tell me they don't think too many women will stay faithful for sentences of 5 and 10 years.

Inmates apparently agree which is partly why they are suspicious, demanding, and controlling of their wives. The conventional wisdom is that if your wife decides to leave you early in your incarceration, at least you can focus on self-improvement and in the long term you will benefit from her decision. Inmates who have spent years trying to nurture a marital relationship while in prison are often devastated when their wives leave them close to their release. They have been "living on the street" and have wasted years of their incarceration thinking about the relationship rather than adjusting to prison and thinking about how to start over. Some men learn of the divorce when they get legal paperwork in the mail, never given an opportunity to discuss the issue with their ex-wives.

Even when the wife doesn't leave, the inmate has to come to terms with the experience of jealousy, the lack of information, and the new power differential that exists. The wife could end the relationship with just a click of the phone or a refusal to visit and there's nothing he can do about it. I have treated a tremendous number of distraught men who express shock at being abandoned, believing in their wives' fidelity until learning they didn't have it. Some men claim they shielded their wives from prosecution but then were betrayed nonetheless. Other men are in complete denial despite ample evidence that their wives have stopped being faithful. Many cuckolded men spend their time worrying, scheming, communicating, harassing, and having family follow their wives in an effort to maintain the relationship. I have heard several phone conversations in which men are making their wives account for their exact whereabouts throughout the day, while they play investigator in an effort to catch their spouse in lies. These are stressful conversations and as the listener you're expecting someone to slam the phone down in exasperation. You're just not sure who.

At the prison, we are all familiar with phone conversations such as, "You say you are alone at home but I thought I just heard some glasses clink in the background," "You sounded sleepy when I called you last night but you said you slept all day," "You mentioned talking to Jill but didn't tell me where you saw her." The tiresome questions and innuendos continue throughout the conversation. Some wives patiently explain their whereabouts while others blow the men off with vague comments and re-directions: "I get tired," "I can't remember right now." Most staff members believe, and I agree, that for their own sanity inmates should stop trying to figure things out beyond what the spouse is willing to share. The sooner he realizes his lack of control, the easier it will be to adjust to life on the inside. Accepting that she is a free agent and hoping for the best is easier than living with constant doubt and suspicion. Then he no longer has to examine letters for hidden meaning, get friends to spy on her, or manipulate his children to learn Mom's whereabouts. Of course, this is easier said than done. Part of the problem is that many of these men cheated and mistreated their wives so there's no reservoir of trust and good feelings to fall back on. What was good for the goose turns out saucier for the gander. In their response to their spouses, wives can be callous or caring, burnt out or with reservoirs of compassion, clear eyed partners, dupes or co-conspirators in the relationship. For the wives, of course, they first have to must adjust to the loss of their spouse, and then cover all the responsibilities that fall on them with their husband's incarceration.

If you want to know the trajectory of support for criminals, track who has stayed on their visiting list after ten years of incarceration. Friends dropped off first, followed by extended family. Wives fell off after some number of years and adult children usually stopped visiting too. Even fathers give up on visitation, probably because of the disappointment, shame, and stigma attached. So who is left? Mom! If you see a 60 year old tough guy finishing his 25-year sentence, it's a good bet that his only regular visitor is his frail 85 year old mother.

When men stay in contact with their family, a source of frustration is their being powerless to help family through tough times. I spend considerable time counseling inmates who want to help but can't. A whole range of serious problems emerge where they are relegated to watching from the sidelines. I flipped through my recent notes for examples: children aren't minding their mother, a spouse is hospitalized, a family member is beaten up by a gang, a parent is evicted from her house, a spouse is descending into drug addiction, a daughter is killed in a drive-by shooting, and children are placed in foster care due to the mother's psychiatric condition. One of the more horrific situations was a man whose whole family was murdered, one individual at a time, possibly due to their being involved in organized crime. Remarkably, he remained stoic throughout.

Some men only imagine they are needed by their family. The family, meanwhile, is too frightened to tell him they want to be left alone. When we monitor their phone conversations we hear the inmate trying to micro-manage problems, becoming angry and verbally abusive when no one follows their prescriptions. In some cases, the inmate doesn't understand the issues, comes up with "criminal thinking" solutions, or takes on a morally superior tone. It's sad to hear the family have to put with it. Men who feel the need to stay engaged with their family need to find alternative roles than "being the boss" or they risk becoming irrelevant and even absurd in the eyes of their family.

The children are invariably the victims. Some children may not even know that their father is incarcerated, only hearing that he is "away," believing he abandoned the family. Others live in sub-standard environments due to the absence of their father or are in foster care and have lost contact. Those who do know have to put up with the social stigma, financial problems, loss, and family tensions that emerge as a consequence. Imagine how difficult it is for children who grow up knowing their dad on the other side of a barbed wire fence. It is hard not to imagine that their views of parenthood, adulthood, government, and morality have all been negatively influenced or seriously conflicted. This is not to say that inmates don't care for their children. Inmates express love and compassion for their children but it is necessarily from a physical and often psychological distance. Many men report that every major life event for their child- making the ball team, graduation, prom night- is a painful event. One inmate told me he was highly motivated to complete the drug program and stay off drugs because "I got people to answer to." When I asked him "Who?" he said, "My kids: they're angry at me for messing up again and I just can't do this to them no more."

Looking at inmates as fathers, one often sees dysfunction. Men who have been incarcerated on and off throughout their adulthood and never had a paying job report they have five to ten children by several different women, none of whom he married. Some men don't know who their children are. Other men only see the children when visiting "the baby's momma." One man decided to relocate to Dallas at the end of his sentence rather than be near his three year old son because "(he) liked the area better." Other men report that although they were the criminals, they were actually the better parent and that their wives are abusing the children. In these instances, we are required to make calls to Child Protective Services so inmates can report maternal abuse. One of the more tragic incidents was when an inmate learned that his wife, who had been smoking methamphetamines, somehow caught the house on fire and that the children got burned as a result. Because there was no relative to provide custody, the children were placed in foster care, which along with all their medical issues was the source of tremendous anguish for him. Wives are sometimes serving time in a female facility for the same offense while men are incarcerated with us. One wonders whether their children can thrive if all the adults in their lives are coming into and going out of prison.

Some apples don't fall far from the tree. A young military man, the son of one of the inmates, tricked me one afternoon. There was a long line of inmate families waiting to be processed on a beautiful April morning shortly after our massive involvement in the Iraq war. This young man, dressed in starched military fatigues, stepped out of line to talk with me privately. He explained that he was being re-deployed to Iraq tomorrow and wanted to see his Dad before he headed out. He asked to go ahead of the line and thereby save more than an hour of waiting. As he put it, "This might be our last time together." My heart went out to the soldier so I went to the processing officer to explain the situation. Fortunately, the processing officer had been working there the whole month and told me, "Sir, I will let him pass if you want me to but he tried the same stunt the last two months." Deceived, I didn't even go back to inform him of my decision. Ironically, as I was walking by the visiting area later, the father called me over to introduce me to his son of whom he was so proud for serving his country. The son was sitting on the picnic bench looking perfectly content, basking in the adulation, but never said a word to me.

Through listening to taped phone conversations, we've been surprised to learn that some family members are willing participants in inappropriate and illegal activities. Some even initiate the activities. We had a woman who recommended to her husband that he cut out the pockets of his pants during a phone conversation. During the visit, she proceeded to put her hands in his pocket and be sexual with him even though there were kids running all around the visiting room. In another instance, we had an adult sibling who planned to put drugs in an empty soda can and throw it into the garbage for cleaning crews to pick up afterwards. We've had many family members including mothers and grandmothers try to bring in tobacco or drugs for the inmates to sell on the compound. For these reasons, officers have to be vigilant in monitoring families who come to the prison.

Inmates sometimes report they worry about their family "ripping them off." Many inmates hid their illegal proceeds by buying houses, cars, and expensive jewelry that they turned over to their families for safe keeping and to avoid listing as personal assets subject to confiscation. They intend to reclaim it when they release. But as one inmate put it, "You never know. Families change over time. You know what they promised you when you went in but you don't know what they'll say when you get out."

On the other hand, even though family members have been dealing with these inmates for years and should know better, they can still be naïve and taken advantage of by their criminal loved one. It is painful to watch family members being manipulated by inmates to violate visitation rules and even risk prosecution. There was the grandma who was urged to smuggle cigarettes in her brassiere, the wife who was convinced to bring in contraband through the baby's diapers, and the mother who wore her son's expensive sneakers that she switched with his cheap sneakers during the visit. A manager here who once worked for Child Protective Services tells me that of the literally thousands of houses she visited in her ten year career, she could recall only one instance where the child refused to open the door for her. This suggests that the children were not learning to recognize dangerous situations. There are spouses who continue to insist on the inmate's innocence. I remember a sophisticated woman who dutifully visited her husband every week with their two lovely children. He was a wealthy man who had been arrested on a sex charge. She supported him throughout his trial and actively advocated for him. She told staff that not for one instance did she believe the charges against him. However, he had been caught on videotape sodomizing a crying six year old boy while on a business trip to a foreign country. No horror brought up in that trial and no amount of evidence could get her to re-consider her appraisal of her husband.

In other cases, spousal members are so beat down by years of abuse that they can't resist the demands placed on them. I remember one wife who had to answer, "yes, sir" and "no, sir" whenever her husband asked her questions on the phone. When she would just say "yes" or "no" to him, he would stingingly rebuke her and make her correct herself. I once saw her with him in the visiting room and they looked like the most normal couple sitting together, enjoying their visitation. It was only by monitoring their phone conversations that I learned the real dynamic. It is commonplace here for husbands to have their spouses visit one day and see their girlfriends the next. They are laughing with both families as if they didn't have a care in the world. You wonder why staff get cynical, but these open displays of betrayal and immorality contribute. Perhaps one of the more obnoxious examples of betrayal I remember was a man who had phoned his girlfriend on her cell phone while she was on her way to visit at this rural location. He patiently helped her navigate her way to the institution, and after a ten minute conversation she was well on her way to arriving. She was a twenty year old college girl about ten years his junior, anyone's daughter going out with the wrong man. The very next day in his phone conversation with his wife, the two of them laughed with each other about this girl's poor sense of direction and mocked her. I had to restrain myself from anonymously calling the girl and warning her about the man she was visiting in prison. He had conned her into supporting him emotionally and financially during his incarceration while she believed he was in love.

Many women look for incarcerated men through magazines and various dating advertisements because due to their low self-esteem they think it is the best they can do. Some women are motivated because they like having someone they can love from a distance without any of the obligations of intimacy that come from real relationships. Other women believe they are getting these men on the cheap, like getting a bargain at a clearance sale. As with many "bargains" there is a reason these goods have been marked down. What these women don't realize is that these grateful, sensitive men who write them adoring letters recalling every detail of their conversations might become more adventuresome, distracted, and independent when they finally walk out the prison gates. Then it's, "Thanks for your support all these years but I have wild oats to sow; you knew who I was when you came into this prison."

A major worry inmates have is of their family members dying while they are in prison. Their lack of control, isolation from family, and inability to say goodbye and learn about the final moments, are etched into those events. The death of a relative is yet another instance where time has moved on without them while they must hide their grief and memories for fear of looking weak.

Perhaps the most desperate requests from inmates is for permission to go to a funeral despite knowing that even if a furlough is approved, they will be shackled, accompanied by guards they have to pay for, and returned to prison right afterwards. Wardens rarely approve them even under the most benign circumstances, like for example an inmate who is due to release in a few months. From a Warden's perspective it's too risky to grant a furlough for something as unscripted and vulnerable to escape as a funeral. Like other intensely emotional requests made of staff, our emotional default position is if you wanted to go to family funerals you shouldn't have committed a crime in the first place. I have always wondered about the reasons for the intensity of an inmate's desire to be at a funeral ceremony, especially since inmates didn't honor family members when they were free. I think part of their motivation must come from deep within the human psyche and in that sense it is more instinctual than rational. I say that because all societies have rituals about burying their dead, suggesting that the response to death and then communication with the spiritual world is deeply wired into our DNA. For the individual inmate, however, I think there are deeply personal motivations as well. First, they have a strong need to be counted among the living. Second, they must manage the guilt they feel that the deceased's last memories of them were of being incarcerated. Finally, they never get to fully grieve their loss. As the next chapter explores, the time that they serve in prison presents many challenges for them while the rest of the world moves on.

Chapter 4

Doing Time: The Psychology of Time

"There is never enough time, unless you're serving it."
Malcolm Forbes

Watchmakers mechanize it and astronomers plot it on calendars while lawyers bill substantial sums for it. Physicists measure it, philosophers explore its meaning, and physicians work to extend it for their patients. Many of us complain we don't have enough of it. Psychologists are way behind the pack since we are just beginning the work of researching its impact on our lives and its meaning. Two recent books on the topic were written by past Presidents of the American Psychological Association. Authentic Happiness[7] describes how to live a better life by considering each of the time dimensions- past, present, and future. Similarly, The Paradox of Time[8] describes how the focus on one time dimension or another impacts our lifestyles. Most of us don't think about time during the day other than to schedule our allotted tasks. Not so for the inmate. When the gavel bangs and the judge orders a hapless man to be in the custody of the state for a determinate sentence, time becomes his constant companion and the most inescapable part of his prison reality.

Time is rarely appreciated. We waste it on inconsequential things; then regret it's passing when it is too late. We look back and catalogue what we failed to do or failed to do well. This is especially painful and poignant for inmates. Prior to their incarceration they never gave time a thought and laughed off concerns about being arrested or "given time." They lived life carefree; they were ripping and running, drinking and drugging, partying in the endless present. They laughed at the "suckers" who worked hard for a living and who saved their pennies in anticipation of a better future. They ignored what everyone told them about good decision-making. They failed to develop skills to prepare for an honest career. They didn't consider that they were squandering their futures.

What a difference incarceration makes. They had no idea they would lose so much, they say. They recall the instances when loved ones tried to warn them about where they were headed. They anxiously anticipate and await their post incarceration futures. They promise themselves they'll do better the next time. They count and re-count their time spent in prison to keep close tabs of the days and months to their release. They feel relief and gratitude for every "day down" in prison because it means they are a "day closer to the door." They comply deferentially with jailors for whom they have no respect and zealously monitor themselves in word and deed so they don't slip up, all so that they can earn back 15% "good time." In an irony some of them recognize, they now face an extremely boring present that they ran from in the free world.

When free, they ignored past and future but now must face them squarely. They re-hash the past and worry about future prospects. Incarceration provided the exact corrective. They now have to re-evaluate their relationship to time. In that sense, their punishment perfectly fits their crime.

In the most famous biblical passage on time, in the Hebrew Scripture's Ecclesiastes 3, we are told:

¹ There is a time for everything,
    and a season for every activity under heaven:

² a time to be born and a time to die,
    a time to plant and a time to uproot,

³ a time to kill and a time to heal,
    a time to tear down and a time to build,

⁴ a time to weep and a time to laugh,
    a time to mourn and a time to dance,

⁵ a time to scatter stones and a time to gather them,
    a time to embrace and a time to refrain,

⁶ a time to search and a time to give up,
    a time to keep and a time to throw away,

⁷ a time to tear and a time to mend,
    a time to be silent and a time to speak,

⁸ a time to love and a time to hate,
    a time for war and a time for peace...

This profound message explains that time is connected to all of life's events. The text informs us that we can accomplish everything we need to accomplish, that our lives can be full and meaningful, and that we can be engaged in the important activities of a full life but there is a caveat. It reminds us there are restrictions. We are free to pursue activities "according to their seasons," which is to say we can't force life to conform to our schedule. We have to engage in activities with humility, when appropriate, and in synchrony with the laws of man and nature. We have to be patient. Unlike modern day prophets, it doesn't tell us we "can have it all" and push us into manic, dangerous "carpe diem" moments. While it is hopeful with the implication that there is a time "for everything under heaven," it is also cautionary with the message that there are windows of time available, appropriate times, and that one must conform to the seasons and rhythms of the world around us. There is a "time to be silent" and a "time to speak" but these are not one and the same time. What happens to people who are reckless, who don't recognize that they must pursue the proper course, who "hate" when they should "love," or who start "war" when they should be making "peace"? There are real consequences. Interestingly, the biblical text in the next passage describes one such real consequence relevant to this topic: the time for punishment.

[16] And I saw something else under the sun:
In the place of judgment—wickedness was there,
in the place of justice—wickedness was there.

[17] I thought in my heart,
"God will bring to judgment
both the righteous and the wicked,
for there will be a time for every activity,
a time for every deed.

The promise that the wicked are brought to justice might serve as a deterrent. For those who remain undeterred, who exercise poor judgment, society has developed the means to bring such people to justice. It's called prison and it's my responsibility as a psychologist to explore what the wicked get out of that experience.

In modern times, with rare exception our answer to what constitutes punishment for law breakers is simple: we incarcerate them, nothing more and nothing less. You could say we use no more sophisticated or cruel a punishment than what we apply to our own children, since incarceration is essentially a prolonged time out. The primary pain is in separating the person from his surroundings, reducing his opportunities for interaction and stimulation, and communicating disapproval. I can tell you as someone who has administered time outs to children and who witnessed the effects of incarceration on adults that it is a powerful tool for both children and inmates. It might seem benign to those not going through it but the punished know it is heart wrenching. Yet compared to a child's time out, the experience for the inmate is much more painful.

While kids get time-outs that are measured in minutes, adults get time-outs that last for years. While kids are given parental guidance about managing the future and must dialogue with parents on their good intentions and how to avoid problems, some adults are released from prison and handed their suitcase without ever having received programming. And while children learn in an environment of respect and support, adults are incarcerated in sterile, sometimes hostile surroundings. If we want prisons to be correctional facilities where inmates learn from the experience, we have to make improvements. In fact, I think prisons can borrow some lessons from the child rearing technique of time-out. In addition to being punished, criminals should receive continuous interventions both during and after incarceration so that they walk out the gates chastened but even more connected to the society than when they entered. They should leave prison determined to live a better life with a skill set that will permit them to be productive citizens. Ideally they should leave feeling more committed to people for having been corrected, and grateful for the opportunity to have a second chance to make good in their community. We shouldn't punish these men without also doing everything in our power to change them for the better.

Valuing each time dimension

Before talking about the inmate's sense of time, let's briefly explore the value of each time dimension, past, present, and future for all of us. Each time dimension has something to offer as well as inherent risks. The past serves as a teaching tool but can also cause us to get stuck in a passive, depressive funk. Best used, the past teaches us the value of family, community, and country; the importance of accumulated knowledge in the world; and lessons about avoiding future problems. The present is our arena for action, observation, enjoyment, and preparation. That suggests taking reasonable risks, seeking pleasure and engagement in the world, meeting challenges, observing others, observing ourselves, and developing friendships, hobbies, and routines, can all be accomplished. Problems occur when we take excessive risks, engage in negative behaviors, abuse drugs and alcohol, and hurt ourselves or others. The future is our guidepost by which we plan what we want while not becoming overwhelmed by the possibilities. In preparing for the future, we can imagine what it will look like, find mentors who are living our potential future, relate to older family members who might experience our biological future, and marshal current resources to prepare for future challenges. By considering positive future outcomes and then working towards them, we create a positive cycle. We nurture hope and optimism to fuel current behaviors, and choose current behaviors to make our futures more hopeful and satisfying.

Multi-timing

Multi-tasking was a fad that supposedly would help modern man solve his time problems. I hope people didn't take it seriously. It never worked for me, anyway. I can't have a good conversation with my children while reading the newspaper and I can't get my professional work done while listening to music. For me, dividing my attention that way is distracting and inevitably produces bad results and hurt feelings all around. There are plenty of dangerous "multi-taskers" out there, like drivers who insist on using their cell phones and decision makers who barely attend to the briefings they receive. Rather than multi-tasking, I have a different recommendation about time. I believe in something called "multi-timing", which is to say valuing and considering all the time dimensions both in daily activities and in major life choices. In fact, I think "multi-timing" (I'm making up the word) is a more productive way to approach most tasks. Look at how it would impact both daily activities and major life choices.

Daily Activities: At first glance, consideration of all three time dimensions in any one activity seems like an impossible standard but it's more natural than you would think. Two quick illustrations make the point: one about coaching a child's sports team and the second about responding to a bad grade on a test.

1) When you volunteer to coach a child's sports team you naturally are involved during the course of a season in multi-timing without knowing it. You are aware of your team's (past) limitations and history by knowing how they got beat in previous games. You evaluate the (past) performance of the team you plan to play next. You practice with a sense of enthusiasm and with all the energy you can muster (in the present) to repair the weaknesses of your game, develop muscle memories, and build on your strengths. You instill hope into the team that they can do better (in the future) if they devote themselves (in the present) to your prescribed course of action. You work toward and visualize (future) success, which is winning the next game, by preparing a strategy (to implement in the future) taking into account the strengths and weaknesses of both teams. Notice how you are working on all three time dimensions simultaneously and strategically in getting your team ready for the next game.

2) The same thing occurs throughout our school years. For example, we receive a low grade on an exam. We recognize that our (past) performance was not adequate. We analyze our

(past) study habits, our study materials, and our test-taking approach. We mentally correct (past) errors and evaluate what parts of (past) class discussions we least understood. We (presently) study harder or differently to take into account what we've learned. We talk with the teacher to better anticipate (for the future) the test we will take and possible test questions. We cancel (future) leisure activities to schedule sufficient time for study. This approach inevitably yields positive results. It comes naturally to us because we have done it our whole lives: learned from the past, attempted to anticipate the future, and implemented changes in the present.

Major Life Choices: Just as with daily activities, we should consider each time dimension consciously when we are making major life choices, as for example in choosing a mate, an occupation, a permanent residence, and raising a family. Failure to do this results in problems that are harder to shake off than a bad test grade or a losing game of basketball. The principles, though, are the same. As with daily activities, one has to learn from the past, make productive choices in the present, and try to anticipate the future. And as with daily activities, many of us do this out of habit. Criminals do not. Choosing the right occupation is certainly one of the bigger life decisions we make and there are significant consequences should it go wrong. We could hate the job, we could be dissatisfied with the pay, we could be really incompetent, or as in the case of criminals, we could select an occupation that will get us incarcerated. Compare the job selection process for both an honest person and a criminal.

Job Selection Process		
	Normal	**Criminal**
Past	• Enjoyed activity • Success with activity • Satisfactory rewards	• Individual had past failures in activity with police, family, authority
Present	• Presently enjoys spending time engaged in it • Discusses it with friends and family • Feels adequately compensated	• Spends time avoiding activity rather than "working" • Dislikes the activity but likes hard work less • Job involves considerable risk that could result in his getting killed or arrested • Individual must lie about the job to decent family and friends
Future	• Individual anticipates continued work in field • Foresees sufficient compensation considering market conditions • Respects mentors in the occupation	• Fearful and ashamed in criminal job • Must stay underground • Acknowledges job is a losing proposition • Promises will quit after "big job" but knows it won't happen. • Knows others in job all eventually get arrested

Summary: Most people naturally inhabit all three time dimensions simultaneously when they are trying to be strategic about improving their situations. One of the failures of criminals is precisely that they make bad judgments about what the past is telling them, poorly utilize their present, and compound it all with bad decisions about how to prepare for their future. More often than not, they fail to consider each of the time dimensions. Instead, they stay rooted in looking exclusively at the present, primarily considering how to have fun in it. Suggesting that we give consideration to each time dimension in our daily lives reduces some of the poor, impulsive decision making in which everyone, but especially criminals, tend to engage. Teaching criminals this fundamental truth would contribute to their success.

The single time dimension: Although I have been focusing on the concept of "multi-timing" there are instances when you enjoy single time dimensions. Life isn't fully scripted. There's tremendous satisfaction from remembering the past for the pure pleasure of it. It's also reasonable to reward oneself in the present after a hard day's work. There's an 80-20 rule: after 80 units of work, reward yourself with 20 units of fun. Similarly, fantasizing about the future stimulates creativity but does not necessarily have to be a part of some problem solving process. When used creatively, it can provide insights or deepen our understanding of current concerns or future aspirations. My point is not that one cannot enjoy single time dimensions but rather that in the broad scheme they should be integrated and complementary.

Time in prison

Prison affects the way a man looks at time in both anticipated and unanticipated ways. Given how indifferent criminals were to the importance of time, perhaps prison will provide them the needed corrective for headstrong lives. When criminals learn to see time differently through the lens of their long incarcerations, they might ultimately develop better preparations and optimism about their future.

Reflecting on the Past:

People like to reflect on their past with an eye toward reconciliation. We want to feel a sense of accomplishment. Of course, people value activities differently. Some people are more proud of having raised children, others at their creativity or work output, and still others at the kindness or help they've bestowed on others. The overall sentiment though is one of looking back and concluding, "It was good" or at least, "It was good enough." Most inmates who are honest with themselves can't have that experience. They failed, they lost, they have nothing to show for their efforts or they recall the hurt they caused those closest to them. They may have neglected their children then compounded it by a long incarceration, they might have been involved in anti-social rather than productive work for which they are ashamed, or they might look back on a series of hedonistic experiences that left those closest to them damaged and rejecting. When judging their own past actions, they experience a sense of failure and each honest look back brings them fresh doses of hurt and regret.

When most of us reflect on our past we feel proud if we at least fought the good fight, tried our hardest, and was true to ourselves, even if we might not have accomplished everything we set out to do. It is how we mitigate the pain of failure- we positively link our current whole selves with the striving person who existed years ago. Regardless of the outcome, our efforts speak to our core values and can be a source of pride when reflecting on our lives. It can also be the source of inspiration for ongoing pursuits. We want to find the thread that weaves from our past into the present in a sensible way, communicating meaning and mission, highlighting the lessons we learned, and perhaps suggesting how to proceed. For example, the man who is approaching retirement might re-kindle an interest in community service that he had to forego during his wage-earning years. Similarly, a woman whose children have grown might pursue creative interests or other forms of self-expression from her youth. In other words, as we age we search for a consistency and continuity between past, present, and future which express our personal interests, attitudes, virtues and strengths.

Look at what happens to the criminal when he initially attempts that. He might look back on a past filled more with behaviors that he is ashamed of rather than interested in pursuing. It is extremely difficult to experience a sense of integrity when our past is rooted in selfishness, our acts were destructive, and our bridges to the people who matter in our life were burned. What strengths and values do we fall back on? What positive goals can we take with us into our futures? Instead some of these men have to think in terms of clean breaks and fresh starts. Rather than continuity, some inmates need to seek discontinuity. It is not as easily done.

Finally, another way that we use the past is by creating milestones. It's a means to catalogue what has happened in our lives by identifying major incidents, establishing timelines, and reliving poignant moments. "I was living in Florida when we had our first child." "I remember the day I got my first job." "The last time I saw my sister was at my niece's wedding." In fact, inmates spend many sleepless nights recalling the past and putting the pieces together in how they got where they are. They are cataloguing their free world experiences to make sense of it all. But there is no counterpart for that experience about the time they spent in prison. For inmates who have done 10 or 20 years they have no easy way of reflecting on all the thousands of experiences they lived through while imprisoned.

When I interview inmates at the end of their incarceration they provide very few recollections about prison life. Partly it's because they don't want to remember. But it's also because there were so few milestones to help them identify important events. They experience prison as a lot of boredom punctuated with frightening incidents. They can't link the important events in their families' lives since they weren't there. Nothing remarkable happened to them inside the fence. What one inmate told me is typical, "Time was empty here. When I look back on prison I can't remember anything because every day was the same. I can tell you about one normal day in a lot of detail but not much else." Without milestones of significant life events, it's difficult to mark time. Their memories of incarceration are bare.

Inmates' sadness is appropriate, not morbid nor necessarily unhealthy. As therapists, we don't challenge these feelings. We allow them to feel deep regret, cry about their wasted lives, and have them use it as a spur to self improvement and rehabilitation. Regardless, it is a bitter and painful pill they must swallow.

Living in the Present:

Have you ever had a moment that you wanted to last forever? We call this savoring and it happens in lots of circumstances- a first kiss, a perfect dinner, the smell of the ocean. In prison, men don't report experiences to savor- quite the opposite, they try to finish time off. Two young men were playing chess with some intensity in front of the housing unit one day. When I asked, "Who is winning?" one answered, "We're both winning." "How do you figure?" I asked puzzled. "We just killed time," and the other nodded. For these young men, time was their enemy and their hope was to defeat it. I generally ask inmates at their final interviews if they ever experienced a moment in prison they would like to savor. Inevitably I get a blank look on their faces. I can see that they want to contribute to the interview but these accomplished con men, usually glib in answering questions, can't seem to dredge anything up. Finally they offer me memories from before their incarceration.

National research shows that waiting is one of the activities people most complain about, whether it is supermarket lines, doctors' appointments, or traffic. Yet no one has to wait like an inmate. In a prison, every activity, no matter how insignificant, often has to go through several layers of review. Remember how I described prisons as places designed to be inconvenient? It takes its toll. Without access to the internet and without full access to the phones, with restricted visiting, poor writing skills, and a lack of privacy, while facing a huge bureaucracy that involves many layers of review, the inmate's sense of purpose and progress gets stifled. Activities that we would arrange in a minute might take an inmate several weeks of diligent work to accomplish.

One inmate who was on trial for aiding a terrorist organization had all his mail carefully screened by the mail monitors. Any letters with Arabic writing on it were sent for translation. The outcome was that he might have to wait several weeks for mail to arrive to his child and then several more weeks to get a response back from his child. Knowing bureaucracies as I do, I imagine that the actual review took seconds but the letter was delayed because it sat on various desks of various departments for weeks at a time as it slowly worked its way through the system. The inmate assumed it was getting carefully reviewed by terrorism experts looking for secret codes and upset his children hadn't heard from him. Would his anxiety be assuaged by the more realistic, but mundane explanation? His priorities are not important to the individuals in a bureaucracy since we have to follow procedures. It makes little difference to us, his jailors, whether he feels impatient or not.

Some of us get a thrill from rushing around during the day trying to accomplish our tasks. We look forward to rest and relaxation because our present existence feels intense but meaningful, pressured but important. Inmates can't relate to that. Rather than the experience of working hard in the present for some better future, most experience nothing happening with few expectations for improvement. The monotony and passivity of incarceration makes time crawl. Every hour feels painfully drawn out. These men often had particular problems with boredom anyway and developed active, thrill seeking personalities as a consequence. Now they have no substitutions to distract or entertain them. One inmate told me that for him incarceration was, "Like watching water boil, day after day, year after year."

Some special circumstances make time in the present even harder to tolerate. Many inmates who were able to make it on the yard decompensate in the hole. The relative social isolation, the cramped quarters, the lack of activities and distractions, and the heat all contribute to their agitation. Some report they feel they are going insane. Others politely ask you not to talk with them because when people ask how they are but can't release them back into general population they get furious. One inmate explained, "Don't ask me 'how are you?' cause you know I'm m**f*ing crazy right now." He meant it and we gave him the space he needed. Some inmates hate every minute of their incarceration. This is hard time.

Many incarcerated men experience time as an unremitting longing for the people they left behind. Their pain is genuine and I can tell you that it is hard to listen to them describe missing their families when they are locked in a cell with no phone or no visiting privileges. The only alternative to communicate with family is the mail which they find unfamiliar and sometimes unexpectedly painful. Perhaps they receive a letter from a child asking them to come home or they receive a Dear John letter. Meanwhile, they are in a locked cell with nothing to do but contemplate the mistakes they made. They have to stifle their longing to comfort their children or plead with their wives for another chance. Perhaps there are plans to send him clear across the country further from family for his own protection or due to a disciplinary infraction. When psychologists pull him from his cell to a dingy interviewing room, the man might have tears running down his face while his hands are cuffed from behind which keep him from daubing his eyes. So as we are talking to him we are periodically dabbing his eyes with a rough paper towel or we watch him struggle unsuccessfully to wipe his face dry with his shoulder. In any case, the experience is pathetic. The truth is that he misses his family. He is experiencing a longing with the knowledge that the desired moment can never be recaptured because his children will be adults when he finally releases. Eventually he becomes accustomed to the pain and no longer requests our services.

Inmates also look at the physical changes in their lives. Did they age too fast or was any kindness shown to their bodies? Have they been able to keep their health? Physical aging happens to all of us. Bodies sag, hair turns grey and falls out, and vital organs stop functioning. Having seen the same men for years, I've watched them age. Men enter with a decent head of hair and leave with a bald dome except for the few perfectly spaced implants that had been inserted prior to their incarceration. Men come in with a full set of teeth and leave with a set of dentures. Men lose their hearing or eyesight during their incarceration. Some carry shrapnel in their bodies from their time on the street so deal with intense pains, in wheelchairs, and suffer various other limitations in mobility. There is nothing to be done. Whether the changes have come from normal aging or their reckless lives they age alone.

Men here also must relinquish their vanities because prisons don't permit the purchase of cosmetic products, such as hair dyes, or authorize cosmetic surgery. It can sometimes result in unwanted bulges, blemishes, and growths for men denied surgery for conditions such as hernias, excess skin after major weight loss, warts, discolorations, and moles on their face. One man with unsightly warts on his face who had been down for twenty years told me, "there's nothing in this place I'm afraid of except the mirror." Many men enter in perfect health but develop heart ailments, cancer, hepatitis, diabetes, and other illnesses while incarcerated. Men who entered healthy leave chronically ill requiring hospice care on the outside.

Physical aging is difficult for all of us but especially so for inmates who have nothing to compensate them. Many men enter prison at the height of their physical strength and stamina, and some must leave spent and weakened. They compare themselves to others and ask if they accomplished anything worthwhile at all while their bodies decayed. Long prison terms feel like death sentences, except it is the intermediate years of life taken. When life is finally returned, they can't pick up where they left off. They get just a few discards, like being handed a brown apple with most of the fruit eaten. The years lost can never be returned, the years returned can never be made whole. Many men feel that what was most important to them was taken and they remain bitter.

Of course, none of us can control the passage of time. It is precisely the inevitable ticking of the clock, the dropping of the sands in the hour glass that hastens our productivity and challenges us to find meaning in our lives. But we feel some compensatory measure of control when we can vary the content in our lives or alter its tempo. Inmates don't have that sense of control. For example, whereas all of us enjoy choosing the time we eat and what we eat, inmates have a menu written in Washington D.C. that follows a bi-weekly schedule, served at the same time every day. It is so regular that inmates jokingly set their calendars by it, saying, "Just 8 more bologna sandwiches till my next visit" or "12 more meat loafs and I'm out of here."

Similarly, when free people want to change the scenery, we take vacations or change our driving routes. Inmates on the other hand might spend 20 years viewing the same layout and buildings. Talk about cabin fever. For company, they live with the same men, difficult and set in their ways to begin with, on a regular basis for years. For work they might be assigned to sit on a bench in hard toe boots with their shirt tucked in, without a radio or a book, prohibited from sleeping, waiting to be called for a maintenance repair job like the Maytag repair man without a magazine. Or they have the alternative experience of being directly supervised doing manual labor eight hours a day. Regardless, they have no control over the schedule. Because it is so predictable, instead of enjoying the moment, they hold their noses and swallow it one gulp at a time.

It is hard to get lost in moments that other people create for you. They get counted 5 times per day, 365 days a year for every year of their incarceration. They stand every night at 10:00 next to their bed for 20 to 45 minutes and at 4 o'clock every morning a light gets shined on their face so they can be properly counted again. Lights go out in the housing units at the same time every weekday and weekend. Open movement to leave the housing units is the same 10 minutes on the hour. They can't leave the building in the evening or early morning. If they miss the 10 minute move, they wait for 50 minutes to try again. The rest of us might have a leisurely meal with friends one day then a rushed meal the next to vary the tempo. In contrast, all their meals last about 20 minutes. If they try to sit a bit longer they create a backlog and the officers will start yelling for people to clear the cafeteria for the next group. They experience time as impassive but impossible to ignore, like a constant weight on their chests.

Flow is a term used by researcher and psychologist Mihaly Csikszentimihalyi, to describe the experience of time passing without awareness due to full immersion in the activity.[9] Most of us feel that we have some activities that are so inherently interesting that we can get lost doing them, that time passes unnoticed because of our intense absorption. This is considered by psychologists to be an optimal experience that produces feelings of real happiness and satisfaction. Rather than enjoying flow, the inmates report having the opposite experience. They find it difficult to engage in any activity with abandon because they have to be conscious of their surroundings at all times. They have to break when they are told to break and there are no exceptions to the rules. They have to be cautious of other inmates who are nearby. It is difficult for them to get the resources they may require or find any privacy. They have to coordinate so many of their actions with authorities that it constrains creativity. Many inmates can't identify a single activity in which they want to engage. I've had inmates wait for me for a couple of hours in the waiting room because I got tied up with an issue. When I come out to apologize to them, they are generally indifferent and say, "No problem. I have to pass the time somewhere- it might as well be here."

Similar to the concept of "flow," people develop routines. It provides us a rhythm that feels right and places to visit at times that appeal to us. Think about your own routines. You've found your favorite restaurant, supermarket, doctor and gym, and have your preferred days and times to go there. You know where and when to get your haircut, a cup of coffee, or take a quiet walk. You know all the highways and all the connector roads and when the traffic patterns best suit your plans. You feel connected to that particular place where you have established a rhythm of activity.

When you've been in prison for a while, your time becomes similarly organized and you can develop a routine in performing your tasks. You know the best time to work out is between 8:30 and 9:30am because some familiar faces are there, it is cool outside, and there is light. You know to hit the showers right afterwards because the orderlies finish cleaning around 9:15am. By 10:30am the microwave is free and at 11:00am the library is clear so you can get ready for your night class. In the afternoon and early evening, you work at your paid job. At 7:00 pm it is pill line so you pick up your day's medicine. You've developed a routine that is satisfying and permits you the minimum amount of stress. It works for you because it matches your needs and wants with what the institution offers and requires. The problem though is that you have little control over how it plays out and other people exert tremendous control over your schedule. We might decide to lock down the units for a massive shakedown. Or an officer forgets to open the doors at a certain time. Or a certain staff member calls in sick and cancels his activity. When the inmates have their schedules changed, for them it is like landing into a strange city. There is a feeling of disorganization and inefficiency. They go to the showers but it is closed for cleaning. They go to the weight pile but the lines are too long so they wait an hour but don't get a turn. They wait in line for an hour and then learn that the activity has been cancelled. At the library, inmates look at them funny for being there and someone is using the reference book they usually use. As one inmate put it, "if they change things on you, your whole day can get thrown off. There isn't a back-up plan because there just aren't that many things to do." That's why these guys can experience such mental distress over something that doesn't seem very stressful for us at all.

Inmates have generally adjusted to prison by the middle of their sentence but might become unhinged as they near release. Usually they are anxious about whether they can be successful starting over with fewer assets and more liabilities than the last time they were out. Most are worried about finances, family, friends, and employment. When you scratch the surface, they describe fears of technology, relating to bosses and citizens, and wondering about their ability to keep up with the pace, demands, and advances of society. They question whether they can perform socially, sexually, and emotionally as they once did with last minute feelings of being unprepared. Will people be able to relate to them or have they changed too much? Are they too hard, too bitter, or too distant to interact with? These are huge fears, but they have no choice. If they have learned anything, they know that time won't stop for them. They will be releasing.

In Psychology we are taught that each phase of life has its own social/psychological tasks that we are programmed as a species to want to accomplish. They are called Developmental Phases. Children are tasked with learning, teenagers and young adults are finding their identity and falling in love, adults are being productive and raising families, and the elderly are imparting wisdom to the next generation. Have you ever noticed that it is particularly sad when an individual is deprived from living out that natural phase? For example, when we see children in poor nations having to work for a living, we are saddened because in addition to the difficult experience, we instinctively feel that they are being deprived of an important and beautiful phase of their life. We are saddened by young people who are forced into a miserable job, compelled to withdraw from college, or are rushed into marriage because we so value and appreciate the freedom and choices that make up that young adult experience. We lament seeing a senior going through dementia precisely because they are at the phase where they should be enjoying and imparting the wisdom they accumulated. That is my reaction to adults who are incarcerated. At a time when they should be supporting their families, contributing to society, and being productive in employment, they are doing nothing but being warehoused. I believe everything in their genetic wiring is propelling them to be productive and generative. In effect, their biological nature is driving them to resist and push against their immutable incarceration. They are being held back from complying with their taskmaster, Time.

What is the antidote? In prison, old inmates advise new inmates to "do your time and don't let others do your time for you". "Doing your own time" means deciding on a course that is useful. It involves developing a plan, turning it into a routine, and then pursuing that routine. There are many distractions in a prison. Staff members make life inconvenient and other inmates try to control him. An inmate who wants to be productive has to imagine what he wants to have achieved upon his release from prison, and start the process of implementing it through concrete activities. He must look at all of the faces of time described above, and make a conscious decision to rise above the pain of hard time, accept it as a demanding partner, relinquish his role as victim, and bend to time's demands, steering his course as best he can. As the biblical quote cited in the beginning of this chapter explained, "There is a time for everything." This is his time for establishing disciplined routines of self-improvement in preparation for release to the outside world.

The healthiest response to the lost time of criminality and incarceration is to use it as a wake-up call. Men who could look back on their errors in the "free world" and make a decision to not repeat them need to cast around for ways of being productive in prison. They can re-establish ties with friends and family on the outside, they can get their GED, vocational licenses, or college course credits, and they could seek mental health programming to make sense out of their problems and strange ways of being in the world. They could become cognizant of their past ignorance about the value of time and decide to take advantage of what the prison has to offer. They can develop healthy habits to take out the gates with them. Their focus becomes self improvement rather than ego aggrandizement, pleasure-seeking, or being miserable. The next chapter, on resilience, will explore this issue in more detail.

Preparing for the Future:

A common worry among inmates is about how much the world will change in their absence. Their children will be grown, their business will be gone, their wives will have left them, and their parents will be deceased. They get depressed imagining a world looking different from the one they left. One inmate was telling another inmate his fear that he would be abandoned during the course of his five-year sentence, saying "I worry my outside world is going to end before I get out."

The other inmate turned to me and said, "I've been here fifteen and he wants me to care about the five he's doing."

People suffering through bad times need hope. They need to know that they can survive this trial and the tide will turn. I find as a therapist that this kind of support is sometimes the most valuable I give, helping people accept that they have to tough it out during admittedly bad times, remain patient, persevere, and wait for life to improve. I believe time heals wounds and it is important for inmates to believe it, too. During tough times people need to have faith that "this too shall pass."

One of the biggest nightmares inmates experience is the prospect of dying while incarcerated. Inmates obsess on this, which inevitably results in their over-utilizing Health Services with neurotic sick call visits. If life were a game, dying in prison is like watching the clock run out while you are in the penalty box. It reinforces the shame, impotence, hopelessness, and frustration one feels at being sidelined in the first place. Inmates are acutely aware that should they become terminally ill in prison there would be no one available to nurture and support them during the physical pain, loneliness, and spiritual turmoil of dying. The only people available would be the prison chaplain, perhaps a "suit" making rounds at the hospital, or a cell-mate- not the people they want near during those final moments.

When we discussed the "present time", we explored the issue of savoring. A similar emotion, also very positive, related to our "future time" is the experience of anticipation. It is like a pre-savoring experience that provides excitement and pleasure at looking to events scheduled in the future. It also tends to be associated with a sense of purpose and opportunity in the approaching days. For example, when we anticipate an upcoming vacation, we combine positive memories of similar past experiences with excitement about recreating some of those same experiences in the future or surpassing them by making a few correctives. However, inmates don't experience much positive anticipation about their time in prison so instead they focus on their release. What is the single most common topic of conversation in prison? What they plan to do once they get out. The problem is that it is years away.

In contrast, upcoming family holidays often become a dreaded reminder for inmates of what they are missing. Events like weddings, graduations, and get-togethers can be a source of pain or jealousy rather than pleasure. Many inmates don't vicariously enjoy the anticipation loved ones go through while they themselves are excluded. What do inmates anticipate at the institution? They are waiting for a table at the hobby shop, a seat in the TV room, or a vocational class to become available. There's not much joy in that. Those who "program" might look forward to starting treatment because it comes nearer to the end of their sentence, taking them "one step closer to the door." The activity itself isn't what is pleasurable, nor would we expect it to be. To the extent they look forward to treatment itself it's because they know it is an opportunity to not recidivate.

Those who are preparing for their futures might not be particularly happy but they are working hard, learning skills they can take with them upon release. They are trying to maintain a good rapport with family members and hoping to return to family with an eye toward genuine reconciliation. They are working on the personal issues that got them incarcerated in the beginning. They are doing what they have to do physically, mentally, spiritually, and professionally to return to their family better men than when they left.

Reflections on Space and Weather

Inmates who are sentenced to incarceration are given both a "time sentence" and a "space sentence." When you think about what a living organism needs, space is as vital as food, water, shelter, and air. Without space, creatures atrophy and die. Research has proven that overcrowding impacts stress levels, fertility, parenting, physical growth, longevity, and a host of other issues. Prisons present a special "space problem" for inmates because of the restrictions of the fences, crowding, and lack of privacy. Some individuals become highly claustrophobic in prison while others become used to the tight enclosures of a cell but become anxious in open spaces. I remember escorting an inmate through the compound who had just spent an entire year in a small cell lock-up. He reported being overwhelmed by all the inmate movement around him. Imagine how he would feel if he had been dropped onto the streets of a major city.

Many men report problems with concentration, sleeping, body functions, and irritability due to crowding. Staff and inmates alike develop a discomfort about having people near them and especially behind them. Criminals who are not content with their space allotment sometimes take the space of their neighbor. Some men have to leave a room when another man enters, relinquish use of the TV rooms, or are forced to live on the top bunk or a different cell. In prison they say "take your space or some one will take it from you".

When inmates compete for the same space the classic fight or flight response gets activated. I've heard African Americans use the expression "in my square" to refer to their personal place. I heard a black inmate tell a huge black officer to leave him alone by saying, "I'm in my square" to which the officer responded, "Not if I go into your square right now and push you out of it". Just as inmates learn to respect time, they learn to respect space as well. They give people the space they need and assertively take the space they themselves require. People who wouldn't accept others' personal boundaries on the outside become acutely aware of respecting boundaries inside the prison. As one inmate put it to me, "The number one lesson I learned in prison is to keep your mouth shut, your nose out of other people's business, and your hands to yourself." Just as with authority, family, rules, and time, the demands of space intrude upon their consciousness and make them sensitive to aspects of life they were able to ignore when given free reign.

When I was a child, I hated all the conversations people had about weather; what it was like yesterday, how it seemed today, what the forecasts were for tomorrow. It seemed to me that people were just pretending to communicate, picking the most harmless, least personal topic they could think about to pass the awkward time available so they didn't have to talk meaningfully. I don't see it that way anymore. When people talk about weather now, I see them trading important information. They are contributing to each other's ability to adjust to the environment. We know that animal behaviors are determined in part by the weather. Migration, sleep cycles, activity levels, hunting, mating, and eating all are influenced by weather conditions. For humans, we know that weather has an unconscious, imperceptible effect on our mood. Men from the

South get depressed by the lack of sunlight in the Northern states. Men from the North suffer during the hot Southern summers. Inmates from Mexico adjust more easily to the Southern climate, while inmates from Texas might find the winters in Michigan unbearable. The latest diagnostic manual used by Psychologists includes the psychological diagnosis of Seasonal Affective Disorder, (SAD) to describe people who develop depression during seasons with less sunlight.

Good prison officers are aware of the weather and make correctional decisions accordingly. For example, when we initially go through a rainy period, inmates become more depressed and lethargic. If the rains last several days, they get cabin fever and might start getting more irritable and rambunctious. I walked into a housing unit one day when the noise level was getting high. The officer in charge acknowledged the noise but defended himself, saying, "Well, it's been raining so much lately that the guys are having a hard time dealing with it. I'm trying to give them a little extra space because the rains will stop tonight and they'll be able to get out more." It worked.

In the wintertime, they are more isolated, put on a few pounds, and sleep more. They tend to keep to themselves to avoid catching colds, which are hard on adults in institutional settings. During the spring, inmates are cheerful and the compound gets chattier. The summers, though, are stressful. When the hot summer comes, the inmates get edgy and you see more tension. They can't choose where they live or work and there isn't always air-conditioning. The "hole" is perhaps the hottest part of the institution at these times with temperatures that easily reach 110 degrees. Inmates are more careful in the summer to avoid misbehaving for that reason. In the "hole" they get extremely irritable but passive. At night they may have to take water from their toilet bowls to cool off the concrete floors on which they'll sleep. They keep the fans running and use evaporation to cool their bodies. Officers help by passing out cups of ice from the ice machine. I remember one hot summer day when the inmates in the hole were highly frustrated by the heat. Then we suddenly got a good breeze and rain, and the mood changed immediately. Everyone went from irritable to cheerful in seconds.

Especially time, but also space and weather, might be thought of as natural phenomena unrelated to psychology, but they play a bigger role in our lives than traditionally acknowledged. They are invisible levers imperceptibly moving our existence. Men who are incarcerated eventually come to understand the special significance of time, space and weather. Before incarceration they didn't worry about engaging in dangerous situations, intruding on another person's boundaries, risking their future freedom or the impact of the seasons. When they come to prison, time comes to a screeching halt, their space becomes radically constrained, and they have less control in mitigating the forces of nature. It forces them to confront past practices. While the rest of the world go about their lives, the men inside initially feel helpless. They can't rely on the old distractions of sex, drugs, risk-taking, bullying, and imagined omnipotence. At first they might try to fight it, ignore it, or laugh it off. Eventually they must calmly stare time in the face because there is no where to run. Then they develop a respectful attitude toward time, space, and weather, accepting its centrality in their lives and yielding to its demands. Ancient man may have understood time better, suggesting that we not overlook our windows of opportunity while also gracefully accepting change. Modern man seems to be wrestling with the issue, hoping that harnessing technology will somehow allow them to escape the demands of time, experiencing stress and frustration in a futile effort to conquer it. Men who lose their freedom, however, can confront their powerlessness over the forces of time and focus instead on making the time they have more meaningful.

Chapter 5

Making it: the Psychology of Resilience

"The inevitable must be accepted and turned to advantage."
Napoleon Bonaparte

I've discussed the shock of incarceration, the social, psychological, medical, legal, and family challenges men face, and the one resource they have in abundance: time. Those are the givens. Despite the problems, some men decide to draw something positive from their experience. Harvard psychiatrist George Vaillant in his book, <u>The Wisdom of the Ego</u>,[10] recounts his research tracking the way men respond to challenges over the course of their lives. He shares that some men can grow up under the worst childhood conditions and yet manage to "right themselves" during adulthood. He calls it "resilience", the ability to bounce back from difficult circumstances and even mature in response to them. Can inmates be resilient? Yes, but they have to be willing to identify the real challenges and make the appropriate adjustments. What are those challenges and adjustments? There are three areas to focus on. There is the brutal underground world of the inmates, the individual's internal world of criminal thinking and living, and finally the opportunities available within the prescribed world created by staff. To succeed, all three areas need to be addressed. How do they tackle them?

Initially, inmates need to emotionally adjust to the reality of prison. That means observing, accepting, and then adapting to difficult surroundings. It means they reduce their involvement in the interpersonal tensions that exist. After they've made that adjustment they can begin the process of letting go of the criminal attitudes, beliefs, and values that brought them to prison. It also means adopting the attitudes, beliefs, and values of "straight" or "square" people. That includes developing constructive routines of self-improvement available within the institution. While no one wants to be in prison, it has to be re-framed as an opportunity to radically change one's entire life. This chapter is about how some men adapt and then change despite the stark, even hostile, prison environment.

Phase One: Adapting to Prison

A common response from inmates when asked "How are you doing?" is "Making it," by which they mean adapting. It might have taken them years to reach that point but it is a watershed event. They've let go of some of the shock, fear, depression, and other negative emotions that have been overwhelming them which allowed other emotions to surface. They figured it out for themselves, got good coaching, or knew how to survive from past experience. Whatever the case, it didn't come easily and it can't be taken for granted. "Making it" means not just righting themselves emotionally, it also means staying out of trouble and adjusting to the institution. In inmate parlance they are now doing time "the easy way" and no longer doing it "the hard way", no longer caught up in all the problems and conflicts that exist here. In addition to surviving they found some measure of psychic peace within the confines of a tough environment that has both indifferent jailors and calculating predators. They "accepted the inevitable," as Napoleon recommended. There are a lot of specific acts a man entering prison has to do to "make it" in the prison but the essential ones involve setting boundaries, showing respect, avoiding troublesome inmates and situations, keeping a low profile, and developing some measure of personal humility.

First and foremost, you have to deal with the underground world of inmates. To make it with other inmates you have to establish boundaries to avoid becoming a victim. Given the mindset of predators, and the reality of prison, there is the risk of sexual assaults. This has to be at least a fleeting concern of every man the first time he walks inside the gates. Men need to make sure that their physical profile doesn't give anyone the impression that they are easy marks. They need to keep their hair short, work out to build body mass, and carry themselves with quiet confidence. Men who arrived in prison skinny with long hair and a hangdog look got bad counsel and most certainly didn't do their homework. I am not trying to blame the victim but rather am advising people on how to deter predators. In addition to making physical adjustments, men need to demonstrate a willingness to defend themselves if anyone tries to confront them. Sometimes that means they have to confront inmates when there are misperceptions that can get them hurt. If they are perceived as weak, they will be treated that way. They need to be "doing their own time" and "not letting others do their time for them." People who don't confront this issue directly will lose their possessions and potentially their autonomy.

More sensitive souls will definitely need to lose the mannerisms, vulnerabilities, dependencies, and expressiveness that might label them as possible sex partners. Sometimes it's as cliché as allowing their voice to drop an octave and speaking more slowly and deliberately. They need to avoid discussions about sex, and not show ambivalence or hesitation when homosexual behavior is discussed. Better to walk away from that conversation, express disinterest, or even revulsion, than to joke about it. They must be alert to potentially compromising situations by not accepting gifts or favors which probably come with strings attached. They shouldn't trust people they don't know or accept friendliness at face value. These guys are criminals, not summer camp buddies. They need to avoid drugs and alcohol because it makes them vulnerable to assault, stay away from unsupervised or poorly lit areas, keep out of other people's rooms, and watch what they tell people. Simple lapses can get magnified into pretexts to be assaulted. They should trust their instincts because situations that feel dangerous probably are.

One inmate told me that early in his incarceration another inmate walked up to him, waved his hand and said, "Let me holler at you, bro." Naively, he followed him right into his room before he realized that he was being pressured. The other man immediately had his powerful arm around his neck and started forcing his head down to perform sex. He pushed his way to the door frame and with an anger and vehemence that surprised even him he yelled at the guy, warning him never to try that again. He avoided that scrape which could have gone very badly and has since learned the lesson which he summarized by saying, "there is no reason to ever follow another inmate where they want to take you."

It's also important for inmates to learn not to draw unnecessary attention. Stay in line, maintain good hygiene, follow the rules, learn the customs, and don't complain too desperately because it's perceived as weakness. One of the psychologists here advises, "Save the drama for your mama." An inmate says you learn to follow your particular institution's inmate rules. At his last institution he learned that new inmates don't have designated floor space for their folding chair in the crowded TV room so they need to watch the TV standing up in the back. He says many new guys learned the hard way that you are better off following that crazy rule than bucking it. So he watched TV standing up in the back of the room like all the other new inmates did, waiting for the old-timers to transfer from the building or release from prison so that he could inherit their spot. When it was his turn based roughly on seniority, he was allowed a space to put his chair. It took eight months. Once he had his spot, he became as protective of the rule as all the other men sitting down because as he put it, "I earned it with my patience and sore feet".

At almost all institutions inmates will probably learn that they need to stay with people of their own race and that they have to avoid sex offenders or they will get labeled. They might learn that the "short timers" are to be avoided because they haven't paid their dues and they stir up too much jealousy. If they can avoid getting caught up with gangs, they are fortunate. They will certainly learn to respect the prison hierarchy, which might mean that they cannot talk to certain people higher up on the social ladder, like "shot callers", without going through their underlings. Depending on the prison, they might have trouble socializing with people from different cities or states. Generally, they need to learn to fit in to the institution's particular rules.

In addition to all the thugs and shake-down artists, prison probably boasts the largest collection of plain out obnoxious characters anywhere in the world. They range from the highly toxic personalities whose back stabbing, rumor starting, hate mongering, and ridiculing ways bring misery to all those around them, to the mildly annoying people whose selfish, rude, teasing, or filthy behaviors seem ripe for an intervention. A colleague describes them as people with "button radars" who know how to find your buttons and push them. They can be anywhere in the institution and they can be encountered at any time of the day. We always counsel men to keep away from them or ignore them. Whether the underlying problem is insecurity, anger, jealousy, arrogance, misery, or ignorance, one shouldn't take their level of negativity personally, and there is no reason to become toxic by association.

Some inmates get so offended and caught up with an interpersonal problem that it becomes their mission to cut through another inmate's difficult personality features and try to change them - a bad mistake. Many devoted people including parents, teachers, and friends have already tried and failed. The best advice is to not react emotionally to these frustrating personalities because it will inevitably exacerbate a tense situation. The offended inmate should take a step back, stay calm, listen to the negative character's perspective if it is being shared, state their own point of view calmly and clearly, and look for areas of agreement no matter how difficult. It's important to keep a positive, civil attitude without caving. Accepting the negative personality style as a given and keeping to one's own agenda is the best prescription. There are few good choices so the best choice is to stay away.

So the inmate trying to avoid problems has his guard up and thinks he should be safe. But criminals are experts at using all sorts of appeals to both positive and negative emotions to bypass a person's protective barriers. If an inmate wants to be "one of the guys," they will buddy up to him. If he prefers serious conversation they will talk seriously with him. If he is anxious, he will be reassured. While some of these behaviors in and of themselves are not a problem, it could be just the prelude to taking advantage of him later. Inmates need to be aware that just because people are getting closer, it doesn't mean they can be trusted. It's best to keep a safe distance at all times until you know enough based on multiple perspectives and not just your own. Inmates will say to each other "Just give me my 50 feet," which is the American Correctional Association standard for the total amount of space each inmate is entitled to in a prison environment based on recommended population density. In a practical sense, I don't think you can ever get 50 feet of privacy. But the expression serves as useful shorthand to describe the constant emotional distance inmates like to maintain.

An inmate on the low end of the social totem pole complained "I have to respect everyone but no one has to respect me." In the world of prison, being civil doesn't guarantee a civil exchange. But it's still the safest policy. I recently witnessed a devastating assault with long-term consequences when an inmate inadvertently got water on another inmate by shaking water off his food tray. Instead of apologizing, he blew off the problem by just shrugging his shoulders when he was confronted, which fed the rage and misperceptions on the other side that resulted in a fight. It didn't turn out well for him. We encourage inmates to learn about simple courtesies and to give respect. We tell them that if they bump into someone to say "excuse me," if they drop something on the floor, to pick it up, and if they inadvertently take someone's spot in line, they have to relinquish it. They shouldn't move other people's stuff without permission, even if it is placed in a public area. They have to be perceived as acutely aware but not necessarily anxious about the possible sensitivities and over-sensitivities of others. Some inmates have chips on their shoulders, perpetual bad attitudes, and they are looking for a reason to fight. They need to be particularly aware of such inmates, called "riders", who will go to war over anything in a bid to be respected.

They need to avoid conflict by listening to what others have to say, making eye contact and not interrupting. They have to use their body language to convey respect by facing people directly. They have to use a tone that shows calmness and awareness of their environment. They must remember that after letting loose an angry or disrespectful comment it is out there and impossible to take back. It is better to look a person in the eye and not say a word than answer with a smart remark that they will have to live with throughout their incarceration. Is this a tall order? Sure it is. But eventually most men get it or lead a compromised existence. If they start out at the high prisons, staying out of trouble will get them to the lows where they can enjoy more psychic peace and the opportunity to focus on different issues.

Inmates also have to get their house in order. They need to keep their rooms clean, follow the rules about the dress code, and not get into negative habits brought in from the outside. Problems in any of these areas will also draw unnecessary negative attention. Many inmates continue gambling habits in prison, a bad idea. Inmates can become beholden to the gangs who run the gambling rings in prison. That could be bad for your physical health. It is also bad for emotional health. Gambling can be an addiction like drugs or alcohol in that one is seeking out the "high" of winning while using it is a way to avoid dealing with other, more painful negative emotions. Generally, inmates must avoid being in proximity to trouble. Inmates who want to "make it" learn they have to be careful about even the appearance of illegal activity. If they hang with rule violators, they will be treated as a trouble- maker so it is better to change associates.

Inmates have little control over what goes on inside the prison and much less about what goes on outside. They cannot control false rumors, prejudice, indifference, rudeness, and criminality on the compound. They also have limited control over people on the outside creating new lives without them. The best strategy is to let go of what they cannot control, focus on their current existence, and work that plan. Guys who were worried about their families, worried about the long term effects of being in prison, or scared about releasing had to let go of the anxieties by just focusing on the day right in front of them and making that one day successful. It's a smaller world now and a smaller life and it's best to come to terms with that.

Similar to "letting go" is accepting "you're in prison, baby. It's a whole new ride" as a lieutenant used to tell inmates who brought minor, unsolvable problems to him. Better to laugh at absurdities than to cry or complain. Prison is not funny but certainly inmates find ways to bring humor inside the gates. When inmates show a sense of humor, or become a wry observer of events, they are adjusting. What are some of the funnier things I've recently heard? An inmate who had his

Playboys confiscated because he had exceeded the limit of 3, mock complained, "But, dude, you know I like to date lots of girls." An inmate complaining about a staff member who he thought was lazy said, "Man, if I had known about jobs like the kind he has, I would never have become a criminal." An inmate complaining about some other inmates said, "They are non-believers and underachievers." An inmate lamented, "You get what you pay for, not what you pray for." Another inmate rhymed, "I'm broke as a joke." An inmate denied having poor hygiene saying, "I may be a criminal but I ain't no low life." A gay inmate aspiring to be a stand up comic wrote this joke: "Did you hear about the gay dwarf? He finally came out of the cupboard."

Inmate nicknames are a constant source of humor and can be directed at staff or other inmates. A hyperactive female officer was nicknamed, "Mustang Sally" from the rock song about a fast moving woman. A no-nonsense officer was called, "Lock 'em up Lupe" - he promoted the nickname because he thought it served as a deterrent. An inmate whose last name started with "Mc" caught with a pathetic sharpened toothbrush was nicknamed "Mac the knife". Inmates who are able to ignore and even laugh at the absurdities and irritations of prison life will do a lot better over the long term. Perhaps the most common refrain I hear from inmates is said with irony. When I ask them how they're doing they say, "It's just another day in paradise".

Thousands of men "make it" to varying degrees. If they don't, they get shipped for one reason or another to some other institution where they try again. I briefly describe three men who "made it" in prison, not because their circumstances are exceptional but precisely because they are typical. As you will see, all are resolved to avoid criminal behaviors when they release but note particularly how they "made it" in prison. I interviewed each toward the end of his more than ten year incarceration.

Three who Adapted:

Mr. A: Convicted of assaults, burglaries, thefts, at the end of his 6th incarceration.

"I wasn't the man I could have been."

Mr. A grew up in a poor home with a working mother and many older sisters in Northern California. He met his father once or twice on the streets but otherwise had no contact with him and tried not to give it much thought. His childhood memories are of staying at home with his sisters when his mom worked, being harassed by teenage gang members because he was small and more of a loner, and engaging in petty criminal acts to get the things he needed. He dropped out of high school by the 10th grade, occasionally finding part-time work to get spending money, but gradually relying on burglary and theft for survival. Mr. A never settled down and as an adult he had a string of girlfriends he would live with for brief periods of time until they tired of him and threw him out. He had children from those relationships but has had no contact with any of them. With his mother deceased years ago, his only ongoing relationship with family is his oldest sister who has been like a mother figure to him. He appreciates that she has never turned her back on him during all of his incarcerations and he feels guilty that he has never really been able to help her in return.

His one opportunity was to help her children, his nephews, when they were younger but he failed because he was never around and now they are grown men also cycling through prisons.

His most recent incarcerations in his view are due to his poor impulse control and bad temper. He hopes he has learned to control that. He feels relatively safe in a prison environment but wants something better for himself. I asked him what guys needed to do to "make it" in prison and he said, "First, you have to accept that every day you have the same routine where you are going in circles. Then you have to accept you have a thousand different personalities that you have to deal with-gossiping, gambling, smoking, people doing the same old negative things. You got to avoid those people and stay with your own program. Then you got to know that the police who are being tough are really just doing their job." For him, making it meant spending more time alone, reading novels from the inmate library, and staying close to his unit. He believes he has changed this time and hopes he can make it out in society.

He has learned from his time in the free world that the hardest part for him has been dealing with all the rules and the rule makers. He sees things differently now. "What I learned is that you have to respect authority…that's the big thing. You got to get tired of bucking, that's when you change". This time around he has had no behavioral infractions and has developed a respectful rapport with the institution staff. He wants to take that attitude out with him to the street. He knows from experience that when he first releases from prison he is highly motivated but when he gets rejected from a job or talked down to, he gets angry, quits, and falls back into "the wrong things and the wrong people." Currently soft-spoken and searching for answers, he worries about his upcoming release. He plans to return to live with his older sister, retired now, and hopes she will help him keep out of trouble. He says, "I want to stay out so bad- it's scary." Already in his 50s, he feels this upcoming release is his last chance to make it on the outside.

Mr. B: former retail store owner- twice convicted drug dealer, a month prior to release

"I wanted mine"

Mr. B was retiree age, over 60, when I first talked to him and almost over with his second incarceration, this one for twenty years. By his report he was an honest man growing up in rural Indiana until he was 28 years old, having grown up in a good home with two hard working parents. But by the time he reached adulthood he was an alcoholic as his father had been before him and he secretly drank to keep himself going. By age 28 he had been married 6 years but his wife was dissatisfied and his meager income as an insurance clerk was a source of tension since "we were barely making it." That's when he came upon a scheme with a co-worker to defraud his company. The plan worked and with the money he siphoned off he opened a small retail shoe store outlet in town where his finances improved. However, it did not repair his marriage. Constantly in conflict with his wife, he found a girlfriend in town, which became the final straw for his wife. She left him and when the divorce went through "she got the store." Bitter at his prospects, jobless and broke, he was thinking that everyone else, like politicians and bankers were all "getting theirs" while a regular guy like him never could. He and his girlfriend started using drugs and eventually began selling them to supply their habit. Wanting his piece of the pie, he now saw selling drugs as the easiest way to get it. He knew it was wrong and hated all the deceptiveness it entailed. He couldn't talk openly to his neighbors, worried when he made errors that might give him away, and felt "bad" when he was around honest people. When finally caught through an informant, he felt relief that the lying and hypocrisy was over.

He confessed to everything and accepted his incarceration. He discontinued contact with his ex-girlfriend and decided that after this incarceration, he would go straight. But it didn't work out that way. Once again dead end jobs, a chip on his shoulder, and a feeling of resentment at his circumstances fed his drug habit and eventually his drug dealing. Today, he is still shocked that he fell back into that lifestyle the second time saying, "I guess I didn't learn my lesson although I thought I had." How does he make it in prison now? He said he learned about the rules of prison and the importance of following them. If having fruit is contraband, don't take fruit from lunch to your cell. If a friend is into something he shouldn't be into, find a new friend. He said compliance and staying to yourself is the key to success in prison because "once you are perceived as a negative person, you will get tripped up one way or another." Looking toward his release having no one with whom he remains close, he plans to live by himself in an apartment and find work once he gets to the halfway house. Although he has no job prospects at present, he knows his heart is right now. As he put it through tears, "If I mess up this time, it will be because I made a mistake or wasn't aware of something. But I know I won't intentionally do anything wrong. I just want to be left alone and live the rest of my life out there. I hope I make it."

Mr. C: Veteran and convicted drug dealer, more than ten years into his sentence

"I needed the thrill of Vietnam."

Growing up in a good household in Maryland with loving parents, Mr. C. has no complaints about his childhood. When he turned 18 he enlisted in Vietnam against the wishes of his parents because he felt it was his patriotic duty to "be there and contribute". Secretly, he thinks he made his Dad proud. Airlifted straight into Vietnam he saw non-stop action, destruction and death for over two years. He himself narrowly escaped death on several occasions, saw many good men die unpredictably, and had more than his share of frightening fire fights. It was that adrenaline rush with the life and death consequences that followed every action that he never got over. A highly intelligent, articulate man, he found it difficult to adjust to the changed routines and mundane existence that characterized his life when he returned to the States. His civilian job, despite carrying considerable risks, was a mild substitute for the pure madness to which he felt addicted after "growing up" in Vietnam.

Watching his marriage collapse pushed him over the edge of caring and self preservation and started his descent into criminal activities. Eventually it culminated in a conviction for drug dealing. He is still appealing the conviction and long sentence on both technical and substantive grounds. He has a hard time tolerating his incarceration and spends much of his time "trying to hold on to (his) sanity by reading historical novels, writing fiction, and pursuing his release through legal challenges." His only friends are comrades from Vietnam who keep up with him by letter and occasional visits. By his report, none of them doubt that his Vietnam experiences contributed to his incarceration. Men on the compound see him as a tough man who keeps to himself, respected and left alone. Younger men who seek his counsel can be shocked by his blunt advice which he describes as "wake-up calls". He admits his ultimate goal is to be left alone to pursue his reading, writing and legal work.

Should he get released, he dreams about finding a deserted island where he has no one to answer to and he can pursue his creative interests in solitude. Mr. C. continues to have flashbacks and reports traumatic feelings about his Vietnam experience which he believes contributed to his risk-taking lifestyle back in the U.S. He joined counseling groups with other veterans in prison to verbalize his experiences, get confirmations from others who had been there, and try to let go of some of the rage around his incarceration. He likes the experience of meeting with the other Vets, but ultimately waits for the day when he can be free. This is no life for him to be leading but given what he went through in Vietnam he doesn't think it could have turned out any other way.

Phase Two: Going Straight

Once a person is "making it" in prison he can take a hard look at his lifestyle, past and present. He has to give up his criminal behaviors recognizing it is insanity to expect a better result from the same actions. He has to stop criminal thoughts and attitudes before they initiate a negative cycle of criminal behaviors. Most men need to hit rock bottom before they decide to change. It's progress when an inmate doesn't like the manipulative criminal he sees in the mirror or finally realizes there is no such thing as "a good chain gang" as Johnny Cash once put it. If he comes to the psychology department, we don't just help them feel better- we use that opportunity to promote a change agenda. The key is to be alert for moments when inmates are receptive to our message for self improvement. You never know when someone will decide to go straight.

Probably our most effective means to convert individuals from a criminal lifestyle is through treatment programs. Yet only a small percentage of inmates enroll. Most avoid them. The average inmate might do five to fifteen years in a prison without entering the psychology department after their initial intake interview. There are only two groups- the drug abusers and sex offenders- who have rehabilitation services at this institution but they comprise a significant portion of the inmate population. Offenders can participate in exceptionally well designed one year long treatment programs that other criminals are denied. Even so, many eligible inmates resist treatment. We have to try to convince them to participate. To their credit, some men are interested in self improvement for its own sake. They want this incarceration to be their last one so they finally surrender themselves to a professional opinion and learn what it takes to become an honest citizen. Ideally, more inmates would have treatment programs available to them and more would sign up.

There is good logic in providing programming for drug abusers. The relationship between crime and drugs is a complicated one but undeniable. Sometimes the substance abuse led to their descent into a world of criminality. At other times the criminality led to a lifestyle of abusing drugs. Most of the time, the behaviors fed off each other. This agency's drug program was named a "best practice" by the American Correctional Association. The participants get housed in a therapeutic community where the living environment is devoted to principles of treatment and recovery. They also receive nine months of drug treatment programming that involve three hours per day of group therapy, community meetings, and supportive counseling. The person is continually confronted and supported by his peers as he learns to become a positive, caring, responsible member of his community. Rather than just narrowly focusing on the "drug addict" the whole person is treated. The individual begins to think more maturely, while his behaviors and feelings become more responsible and caring as well.

One of the components of the drug treatment program focuses on their criminal thinking patterns, which we call "thinking errors." Dr. Stanton Samenow, a national expert on the criminal personality, has written several books on the topic and participated in a federal commission about the criminal mind. In his classic book **Inside the Criminal Mind** (1984, 2004) he describes the various thinking patterns that criminals display.[11] Listed below are 8 common thinking errors we focus on in the program.

Cognitive Treatment: 8 Criminal Thinking Errors

1. Mollification. Criminals play down the seriousness of their criminal conduct. They might tell themselves "it wasn't that bad a crime" since "no one got hurt" or they might become resentful when others "make too big of a deal about it." Specific examples of mollification include ignoring how others were hurt, blaming the problems on someone else, making excuses for the behavior, or playing the victim. They might excuse the behavior with comments such as, "everyone in my neighborhood did it- it was called survival" or "if I didn't sell drugs, someone else would." They blame the lawyer or claim they got "set up" since they were only selling small amounts of drugs anyway. When confronted with their crimes they tend to think, "There's nothing wrong with that," rather than reflect on their culpability. One criminal made a living selling "beautiful gold pendants" to elderly ladies on the telephone for $100.00. Once he received the money, he would mail them a gold pendant so tiny that they could barely thread it onto a necklace. He confided that he purchased the pendants for $1.00 but he could not be made to see how his practice was deceptive, even after his conviction for fraud. He was fixed on the idea that he sold them gold in a legitimate transaction and so prosecutors blew the incident out of proportion. This kind of thinking will never let them confront the seriousness of their criminal behaviors.

2. Cut off. Inmates may distance themselves from the thoughts and feelings that would otherwise constrain them from breaking the law. While living an honest lifestyle but perhaps under significant financial pressure, they finally decide that they're tired of the pressure and go out to rob a bank. They ignore all the good judgment and pro-social impulses under which they normally operate. This "I've had it" moment allows them to do what they want rather than pursue more appropriate solutions. Some use drugs or alcohol as an aid to "cut-off."

Some talk themselves into it. A colleague who treats many drug abusing criminals is sure that "cut-off" is the best explanation for why criminals commit crimes. He says he see countless people with normal emotional, familial, and social lives who then go and commit the criminal acts which they genuinely regret for a long time afterwards. He says no other thinking process describes how that happens better than "cut off." On the other hand, many criminals have told me they are unconvinced of the existence of "cut off" and see it as an excuse a person uses to avoid taking full responsibility for his criminal attitudes and behavior.

3. Entitlement. Then there is a grandiose sense of being better than others or more deserving, entitling one to live how he wants without following the same rules of conduct as others do. Rules are for suckers but he is entitled to be above the law. He can take what he wants, he confuses his wants with his needs, he believes that he deserves what others have, and thinks that because he has done without for so long he has "earned" the pleasure no matter how he obtains it. The underlying belief is that he is owed something. One inmate regularly sexually abused his daughter from the time she was aged 10 until she was 17 at which time she reported him. During that seven year span he never once worried about her being victimized or whether what he was doing was right or wrong. Looking back on it from prison he explained, "I was the breadwinner, taking care of the whole family, and I figured that all of them had to do whatever it took to keep me happy." In prison he cried rather openly about the consequences of his having had that entitled attitude. The issue of entitlement comes up with inmates when we discuss with them their employment options. They might tell us, "I can't start at the bottom of an organization because it's beneath me".

4. Power Orientation. The criminal's perspective may be that "being a man" means dominating others. The world is divided up into the strong and the weak, "winners" and "losers", and someone has to come out on top. They believe that survival requires them to accumulate power over others and without it they don't feel safe or satisfied. It's the law of the jungle where they would use any tactic to obtain power. They prefer fear to trust because they believe it is more reliable. Money, violence, and weapons are all used coercively to maintain their dominant status. Relationships are seen exclusively through the prism of who's in control, e.g., "no woman is going to tell me what to do- I tell them." These criminals necessarily have conflicts with legitimate authority. For example, "I used to make more money than the guards do, so I don't have to listen to him." This power orientation can also be used to justify any kind of aggressive behavior such as "he's weak so I beat him" and "he felt threatening to me so I beat him." People such as this often have difficulty learning in group treatment because they experience the role of student as putting them in an inferior position and they don't make good listeners.

5. Sentimentality. This is a quality you don't imagine you will see in criminals but invariably you do. They spend so much of their time ripping people off, dominating, and manipulating, that they need something to convince themselves that they are "nice guys." That is the core motivating principle for sentimentality. A lot of criminals will tell you that they gave money away, bought their family great gifts, or are generous to kids in their neighborhood. They are great tippers in restaurants, charitable to some, and very public in their generosity. But these sentimental displays are their way of buying themselves self-esteem on the cheap, without making a life long commitment to being responsible or looking at the implications of their regular day job. Their attitude seems to be, "When I'm hurting people, that's just business but the real me is a nice guy."

6. Super-optimism. Some criminals think they can get away with just about anything. Although there are many good reasons not to engage in crime, most of us agree that at least one of them is that there is a high probability of getting caught. Criminals don't see it that way. They convince themselves that they will walk away clean because they're so clever. They think they can outsmart the police and detectives 100% of the time. Due to their super-optimism, they fail to muster sufficient anxiety to give up on their criminal lifestyles.

Super-optimists don't realize that the percentages are against them since even being caught for 1% of their crimes will eventually cost them 10 years or more of hard time. Instead, their confidence grows as they wrack up their list of undetected and unsolved crimes. Often they tell themselves they are "waiting for one big job" before they quit, but that one big job will never come. How could it? They are mostly low level players who make the same amount of money for each "job" they do. It might buy them a few weeks of peace but it won't allow them ever to retire. Thinking of "the one big job" is another example of super-optimism.

Another frequent super-optimistic idea is in imagining they can control the extent and circumstances of their criminal lifestyle. Here are some of the things they might tell themselves:

- "I'll sell marijuana but not hard drugs."

- "I'll stay away from the bank robbers and hang with the petty criminals to keep off the radar."
-"I can trust the guys on this deal because I've known them for a while."
-"I've driven drunk and high a thousand times and can do it well."
Without realistically appraising the likely consequences of their behavior, criminals have a false sense of optimism that eventually brings them straight to jail.

7. Cognitive Indolence. This describes the tendency for criminals to not think carefully about their promises, futures, and daily behaviors, and to take the easy way out. This individual might promise employers and family that he will make changes "tomorrow", but he doesn't develop any plans to prepare for that "tomorrow". He says he will get to it later. Of course, those who take him at his word are quickly disappointed. Perhaps under family pressure he agrees to enter a treatment program but quits because he believes the material is repetitious and he already knows what he has to do. Or he takes the job but doesn't show up because he's not in the mood and doesn't anticipate that his boss will tire of the absences. These individuals draw the wrong lessons from their criminal histories. At the prison, many of these inmates have concluded "I got caught last time because I was sloppy. I'll just do it better next time".

8. Discontinuity. This involves those who set reasonable and positive goals with every intention to complete them but then fail to follow through. It is cognitive indolence at a later stage of the behavioral chain of events. There is a mental disconnect between their goals and their ultimate behaviors. They might say, "I plan to start looking for work tomorrow" but then they get sidetracked with other events. Or they get excited because the probation officer found them a job but give up because the job is across town. These individuals seem to miss appointments, lose track of time, fail to follow through on commitments, get distracted, and take too many short-cuts to achieve any success. They tend to minimize the work involved in the planning phase and then fail to sustain their work effort when it is crunch time.

We teach the inmates these eight criminal thinking errors and have them practice new, more realistic thought patterns. They analyze problem situations that occur in their lives, first looking at it through the lens of their criminal thinking patterns and then trying to see the same events as honest citizens might. The goal is to help them contrast their own constricted, distorted thinking processes with a more pro-social outlook, and eventually to see the world in a more constructive manner. When they start becoming more reflective, open-minded, and deliberative in their thinking, they recognize the futility of their criminal lifestyle and begin to identify with the "straight" citizens they formerly disparaged. Unfortunately, inmates without substance abuse histories don't receive this program due to resource limitations.

In addition to the drug treatment program, we also have an intensive treatment program for sex offenders. Sex offenders are the fastest growing criminal population in the federal system. Current criminal justice trends suggest that sex offenders will continue to be a rising percentage of the inmate population for many years to come. The public expects them to receive effective treatment so they don't commit the same offenses when they release. Doctoral and master's level treatment specialists work with groups of sex offenders for several hours a week focusing on their honestly divulging problems, developing victim empathy, taking responsibility for past behaviors, forming appropriate relationships, appropriately fulfilling essential human needs, developing more effective emotional regulation, and learning relapse prevention.

In the old days, sex offender rehabilitation essentially consisted of warning sex offenders about all the ways they can get in trouble and threatening them with further incarceration. It was not a particularly effective message. It was essentially giving them a list of things they could not do, but without suggestions about how to live their lives. The result tended to be that they withdrew from decent society and went further into a criminal underworld of people who shared their perversions and problems. Current treatment approaches are more sophisticated and effective. The focus now is for the criminal to accept his need for sexual relationships, social interaction, recreation, and pleasure. He is encouraged to see these needs as normal, traditional desires but then learn appropriate, legal means to satisfy them. It appears these groups will be a more effective means of treatment than has been provided in the past but, of course, much more research needs to be done.

When an inmate lets go of his criminal lifestyle, he takes responsibility for his mistakes. Gone are the evasions and half truths. He got himself to prison and doesn't blame everyone else for his being there. When a man takes full responsibility for his incarceration, it frees up a lot of psychic space that can be channeled into positive activities. Those who want to be victims quibble about the charge, the sentence, the law, the "snitches", the judge's personality, the incompetent lawyers and evil prosecutors but never admit that they knowingly committed a crime. Those who want to justify their behaviors blame their circumstances or exaggerate the pressures they were under.

Inmates not ready to take responsibility get into philosophical discussions about drugs and libertarian principles, incarceration rates in one country vs. another, the prison industry complex, the government's role and constitutional protections against searches and seizures, children's rights and sexuality, and high flown notions of freedom. But they knew about criminal laws and the consequences for breaking them. While they might fool themselves with justifications, ultimately they are the losers by not learning from past mistakes. All the time they spend denying, blaming, and excusing is time that could be spent productively elsewhere. Taking responsibility has practical implications because it helps a person adjust to incarceration. Inmates who admit, "I was stupid, greedy, impulsive, high on drugs or angry" to explain how they landed in prison are healthier and happier many years later.

It is a paradoxical truth that by accepting the most painful, negative aspects of our selves we have the greatest opportunity to grow. It is a process of destruction and renewal. That's why those who have suffered tragedy often see themselves in some profound way as having benefited. Frederick Nietze's observation that "what doesn't kill you makes you stronger" is true if you can learn from the experience. Unfortunately, instead of confronting painful truths about the self, most people prefer a mental "fight or flight" mechanism to avoid it. What they need to do is take responsibility for their bad actions and then begin the process of self-improvement, self-acceptance, and possibly making amends. One needn't be paralyzed by guilt or shame. After taking responsibility a person can embrace the spirit of renewal.

Inmates know better than anyone about whether their legal case is solid. If a serious legal error has been committed and they have been wronged, they need to mobilize their resources and battle for their rights. If they should be serving five years but are doing twenty then it is time to hit the law books. In my experience, this is the exception. In most cases, these guys are guilty but just can't get themselves to acknowledge it. It would be better for them if they did. Rather than endlessly fighting the court system they should use their incarceration as a springboard for personal change. Many mature and successful inmates tell me that while the conviction had unfair elements, they also committed many crimes they weren't convicted for. On some level, karmic justice was served. I imagine that when the defendant, his attorney, the prosecutors, and all the witnesses know the defendant is guilty, the court proceedings take on a surreal inevitability. Guilty inmates not appealing their convictions, like men who take responsibility for the harm they've caused, have the time and energy to prepare more successfully for the future.

Inmates need to incorporate their law breaking behaviors and incarceration into their emerging identity to feel whole. Whether they saw their criminal life as a necessity, a bad occupational choice, a character flaw, a circumstance due to poor parenting, or all of the above, they have to include all the criminal behaviors and their time in prison in their definition of self. They also can't ignore the negative lifestyle choices they made, such as the drug abuse, infidelity, poor parenting, disrespectful relationships, and dirty dealing with others. Some may incorporate their past into a profound spiritual journey where they define themselves as going through the stages of ignorance, loss, knowledge, and then redemption. For those who made a single mistake, it could be defined as an error of judgment that they can recover from in an otherwise exemplary life. In either case, they must be honest with themselves to complete their identity.

Then it's time to focus on other tasks, like improving their physical health. There is no better opportunity than while in prison because there is so much time and few distractions. Men can lose weight in prison, give up bad chemicals, and get so much stronger and healthier so that they actually feel younger during their incarceration. A client of mine lost 80 pounds pushing a lawn mower in his outside grounds keeper job. When the gas powered lawn mower came available to him, he turned it down because the more strenuous job forced him to walk 12 miles each day and kept him healthy. In the long term, men add years to their life during their incarceration. Staff members watch our bodies get soft and pudgy while we wistfully watch the inmates' get strong and trim. A 60 year old does vigorous lifting and calisthenics at recreation and has the body of a 30 year old. It's inspiring to men look so fit at that age. Whether these men exercise to reduce stress, improve their health, satisfy their egos, or attract females upon release, they demonstrate that it is never too late to get in shape.

Just as a person needs to work on his physical health, he can take a measure of his emotional health. It's good to regularly check how they are feeling, search for inner calm, and let go of things they cannot change. Since they are no longer taking drugs, their mental clarity is improving daily. Practical steps to improve their overall adjustment include relaxation techniques, developing an optimistic outlook, striving for positive outcomes in relationships, planning for the future, and developing a sense of appreciation for all that life has given.

There's a lot of idle time in prison because there are too many inmates chasing too few meaningful jobs. It is still their responsibility to find creative ways to occupy their time. They have to avoid tolerating inactivity, watching TV, and wasting time sleeping. Inmates who succeed fill up their schedules - they write letters, keep journals, take evening classes, find hobbies, join sporting leagues, establish realistic goals, and try to lead as balanced and varied a life as possible. As one inmate put it, "When I wear lots of hats at least I'm not raging." Some men figure out that while in prison, all the pressure in their lives has been removed. There are no outside phone calls, no children to attend to, no worries about locking doors and setting alarms, no bills, no responsibilities, no obligations, no cars, no presents to buy, no meals to prepare, and so they have time to relax, think, find contentment and build a life.

Eventually, their lives develop a rhythm that makes the time go faster. Conversely, unscheduled time results in substance abuse, overeating, oversleeping, and tendencies towards laziness or trouble-making. When I am scheduling appointments with inmates, the more mature ones tend to steer me away from certain times saying, "That's when I study" or "That's when I work out". I used to think they were being a bit inflexible or obsessive given all the time at their disposal but I've come to understand that their focus and discipline adds meaning to their lives which ensures they accomplish their goals.

Victor Frankl, a concentration camp survivor and psychiatrist who wrote the book, Man's Search for Meaning, described the importance of finding meaning in one's daily existence.[12] He described how individuals who found meaning in their concentration camp existence developed the psychological will to survive those horrific experiences. For him, finding meaning was as essential and life-sustaining as was finding sustenance. In the prisons, despite often low brow histories, inmates also have to make sense of their experiences and find a current meaning to their existence. This can be challenging when they don't have loved ones nearby and while they are living in a monotonous, under-stimulating environment. Some men use the time to develop their characters while others focus on developing job skills, pursuing academic interests, making psychological improvements, and having creative or spiritual pursuits. Prison is their time to try out new activities, re-orient themselves to what is important in their lives, and hone the skills they can use in their future. Others begin to reach out to help those around them. Perhaps they begin to attempt to lift the mood of others, be a positive role model to the young men, teach the illiterate, or counsel those in trouble. The challenge is to find fulfillment while acting responsibly.

Part of being successful in a prison also involves improving relationships with all of the different people you come into contact with. Because it's such a diverse environment, harboring prejudice and racist sentiment will interfere with anyone's ability to feel comfortable and emotionally whole. None of us developed prejudices in a vacuum. We grew up in cultures that played a part in influencing our beliefs, values, and ways of relating. Many of us have also not have had a lot of experience interacting with people from different cultural and religious backgrounds. As a result, some inmates assume that everyone from another race will react the same way. They may also have developed the bad habit of discounting people from other races as being "ignorant" "hostile" or "too different" before they've even talked to them. For these individuals, it would make for growth to become respectful and open minded when communicating with inmates from different backgrounds. Such inmates will be able to walk the compound with fewer conflicts and can take that successful attitude out to the real world after their incarceration.

In addition to finding some measure of inner peace and some level of acceptance on the compound, inmates need to reach out to family back home and especially to their children. This is no easy task. They have to relinquish the traditional "control model" of parenting which doesn't work from a prison setting. Their ability to stay engaged with their child will depend on them adopting new roles like coach, support system, sounding board, source of interesting information, and friend. They can't be the disciplinarian they once were because they don't have the authority to enforce the rules. When other adults, such as overwhelmed spouses, try to get them to take on that role it can be very intoxicating for the men to feel needed. But in the end it would backfire and alienate them from their children. Similarly, prison is not a good platform to be in the role of moral authority. I've heard lots of inmates preaching to their children about good behavior but the elephant in the room is that he himself didn't behave so well when he had the chance. Rather than lecturing, we tell inmates they need to encourage their children to act responsibly. To facilitate the discussion, they can frankly acknowledge their own mistakes, perhaps not with a full description but at least enough so the child understands the serious consequences that result from bad behavior.

A challenge for inmates is when they learn their child has found mentors or role models in the community. In those circumstances, the father's role is to encourage his children to maintain those mentoring relationships no matter how jealous it makes him feel. While no one can replace him, he cannot perform many traditional activities of fatherhood while incarcerated. That doesn't mean he can't find activities they can enjoy together. Men find games, hobbies, music, TV shows, and other interests to share and discuss regularly with their kids. He can stay interested in the child's activities and work to develop a good rapport. He shouldn't expect long telephone conversations or letters because most children can't sustain that level of communication. He also can't wear his feelings on his sleeves, must accept they will be busy with other activities, and assume they will forget to write. He must stay positive. In the free world, people need to make about five supportive comments to a person for every criticism if they want their comments to be accepted; from the world of prison that ratio is probably higher. He needs to respect the child's mother. He shouldn't criticize her, get children to spy on her, or undermine her authority with negative comments. If the mother is not supportive of prison visits, he can try to engage grandparents, aunts and uncles, or another family member to bring them. If visits are out of the question, he has to rely on phone calls and cards or letters. If he has extra money, he can send stamped cards and letters that they could mail back. He should remember cards on holidays, express affection regularly, and share hopes for contact in the future. For men, supporting his children while working on his parenting skills and character is the best preparation for parenting upon release.

The long term goal of succeeding in prison involves building character. Building character is a lifetime pursuit. It's never certain what will start a man on the right path. Inmates tell me that they wake up every morning shocked and thankful to be alive given all the drugs and violence they had been involved in out on the streets. Many inmates have told me in one form or another, "An addict either dies or goes to prison so I was one of the lucky ones". They experience gratitude, a good emotion to build on. Many men report they have become more humble, open minded, spiritual, responsible or family minded in prison.

I spoke with an inmate yesterday who got his nose broken in several places and had it pushed deep into his nasal cavity from a single punch following an argument on the baseball field. Fortunately, his friends were able to extricate him from the situation and get him immediate medical attention. What amazed me is what this young 23 year old inmate took away from the experience. Even though he witnessed the murder of his brother by a rival gang in a drive by shooting and also saw his heroin addicted father die in a robbery attempt, he never questioned his life as a "gangster." Getting his nose smashed, however, made him give up his criminal lifestyle because for the first time in his life he felt victimized. This led to his feeling empathy for his "baby's mother" who he had hit on several occasions. He then started "seeing through" the egotistical posturing of old friends who were criminal and selfish. Confused by these new feelings and perceptions, wanting to know if there was something wrong with him, I assured him he had taken the first step to emotional maturity. We discussed ways of building on it and developing the character traits of humility and empathy which had been absent in his life. Upon his release from prison one year later, he was determined to be a good husband and father.

Every inmate will have different values and traits to develop. However, most cultures put on a premium on a short list of character traits so there is a ready made prescription for people interested in self improvement. Martin Seligman, in his book, <u>Character Traits</u>, named several that span cultures and times. They include traits such as learning, persistence, courage, caring, citizenship, humility, self-control, and gratitude.[13] To develop these traits, one has to build them into their daily life- it doesn't happen overnight. As an inmate would say as a daily greeting year after year, "one day at a time, one day at a time."

Eventually all these men release from prison and need to prepare for their return home. Men who hustled before they came to prison must use their time planning how to make legitimate money upon release. Men who need an education, a diploma, a license, a skill, a resume, a business plan, a supportive family, a sober lifestyle, or a job need prison time to prepare. While it is difficult to predict the needs of the future and to imagine what society will look like at release there is no better time to start than the present and it can be done from prison. Opportunity knocks when you are hard at work.

Three who Went Straight:

Mr. D: Popular high school teacher and child pornographer. "I had a sex addiction."

As a 15 year old suburban child in Seattle, Washington, Mr. D. knew he had an obsession. He was thinking about sex all the time, wanting to see pictures of women, and it wouldn't go away. He didn't know why he was having these thoughts but he desperately needed the visual stimulation. By the time he got to college and found the internet, Mr. D. would spend hours every day looking at naked pictures on the screen and then spend the rest of his time seeking out girls to satisfy his ever-present desires. Good looking and socially pleasant, he found it easy to find girlfriends and initiate relationships. But as with viewing pornography where you move quickly from picture to picture, Mr. D. easily got bored with each girlfriend, needing to move from one to the next. To satisfy his need for sexual variety, he would manufacture a conflict to justify each break up and in this way kept a constant rotation of girlfriends.

Because he came from a family of educators he decided to obtain a teaching degree in college and he took a job at a local high school in his hometown where he met and married a fellow schoolteacher. Soon they started raising a family to whom he was committed and loved dearly. Although faithful in his marriage, Mr. D felt sexually bored and eventually returned to his obsession with pornography despite periods of abstinence. To hide it from his wife he used a lap top which he kept locked away in his home office. Like many men who spend hours watching pornography, pictures of naked ladies got boring for him and he drifted into other areas. As he put it,

"20 year old women can look like 16. And 16 year olds look a lot like 14. And 14 year olds don't look much different than 12." It was this gradual descent into the viewing of child pornography which eventually resulted in law enforcement's detection of Mr. D. Because internet pornography crosses state lines on a computer's "world wide web," his case was picked up by federal law enforcement. Because he was a school teacher having daily contact with children as well as responsibility for them, he made a great publicity case for prosecutors and would send a clear message to other wrong-doers.

Brewing fresh coffee one morning in his newly refurbished kitchen, he was in good spirits, "loving life," and thinking about an upcoming summer vacation to Canada with his wife and children. He never made it out of the house. They busted Mr. D. in his home, seized his lap top, and immediately incarcerated him. He was denied bail because he was "a danger to the community," and so went from "loving life" to losing everything he valued in a single day. Because Mr. D. was a school teacher his case was splashed across the local news and prosecutors demanded a lengthy sentence. While men in state cases might get less than 10 years for rape or even murder, Mr. D.'s legal team could not prevent him from getting 14 years in federal prison for his first criminal offense of viewing child pornography on the internet. His wife, disgusted by his behavior, left him while his shamed children have no contact with him. This put him in the throes of a depression for which he has relies on his religious faith.

His biggest worry and heart ache is that his young children will barely know him or want to know him when they are adults upon his release. Fortunately, he was motivated for treatment and completed a 9 month sexual offender treatment program. He is a teacher in the night school and other inmates appreciate his excellent style and well organized presentations. He completed treatment to free himself from his obsessions with pornography and to convince his family that he could change. He is hopeful that by having taken full responsibility for his actions and continuing to focus on building positive cycles of behaviors, his family will eventually reconcile with him.

Mr. E: Airline employee and convicted murderer at the end of his incarceration

"What I did was against everything I believe in."

Mr. E. was one of the nicest guys you can meet in a prison. Pleasant, cheerful, respectful, he was liked by both staff and inmates. He seemed to stay positive every day of his incarceration. While he says he could have felt bitterness about the double digit sentence he was given, Mr. E. expressed understanding for the judge's decision and the imperfections of the criminal justice system. Essentially, he was guilty of a crime and had to pay the consequences. Regarding his incarceration, he is grateful for the college courses he received, the vocational classes, and the opportunity to start over at the end of his sentence. Having been in contact with so many inmates over the years, Mr. E. is also grateful for his own family and upbringing which he has come to appreciate more during his incarceration. This all led to his seeing his principal mission while incarcerated as emotionally supporting his family while also bucking up the inmates who live here.

Although his parents live in Florida, too far from the prison to visit him, he regularly reassures them by telephone that it was his own fault and they needn't blame anyone else for his incarceration nor worry about him as he is doing fine.

On the compound, he recently gave stamped Father's Day cards to a grumpy, depressed inmate who had stopped writing his children to encourage him to write. At the time, the inmate reportedly looked at him with suspicion but later came back to tearfully thank him. He also told a young inmate to stop whining on the phone with his terminally ill grandmother and counseled him to provide her support when she is most in need. Because of these acts of kindness, other inmates tell him he is different since "you just can't do what you do in a prison." Mr. E. believes that he gets away with supporting others on the strength of his personality as well as the fear others have for him due to his involvement in a frightening crime.

He grew up in a good home with a loving family in Miami, Florida but when he returned from the Iraq War he wasn't ready to settle down with a wife and kids. He bought his own place, surrounded himself with pets, kept a steady job with decent pay, and enjoyed his close knit family and lifelong friends. Athletic and social, he had loads of surfing buddies and plenty of girls to date. After a work injury, he started using pain pills for the damaged disc and then steroids to rebuild his body. He believes those drugs caused his downfall. Steroids seemed to have a big psychological effect on him, compromising his decision making, making him more edgy and impulsive, not quite at the level of "roid rage" but impaired. The pain killers contributed further to his impairment by giving him a "loopy" high. He admits that he came to rely on the emotional boost drugs gave him because he had become so discouraged with his medical problems.

One day, that cocktail got him into the trouble that changed his life. During a camping trip with friends, an acquaintance asked him to help confront a former corporate customer who reneged on some bills valued at "hundreds of thousands of dollars" and "like an idiot" Mr. E. agreed to go. What he didn't know is that the confrontation would get ugly and eventually lead to a murder. Although he immediately reported the crime, it was prosecuted as a conspiracy and he was a co-conspirator. Prosecutors determined that Mr. E. could not walk or the case would fall apart. As a result, he was forced to plead and is now serving his time. Awaiting his release next month, he would like to start a family but wonders if he is too old and whether he can still find the right girl given the baggage he brings. His closest friends have all married and started raising families which makes him feel out of kilter. His biggest excitement is to be among a community of honest people who basically "respect you and are decent, unlike the guys I've lived with here all these years".

Mr. F: Former stockbroker, convicted of fraud, married and father of 3.
"I was greedy and too proud"

Mr. F was a successful stock broker for much of his adult life. He never had legal difficulties and wouldn't have associated with anyone who did. He considered himself to be a nice guy, a people person who tried his best to keep his customers happy. They rewarded him with loyalty and a steady stream of income. The stock market fared well for the first two decades of his career and Mr. F became successful beyond his expectations. His wife was satisfied living their upper class existence in a suburb of Chicago and they raised 3 well-adjusted girls, all of whom doted on their father. But when the stock market nose-dived in 2001, he and his customers took a "big hit." Rather than admit error about his stock picks and scale back on his lifestyle, Mr. F. committed the mistake he would regret throughout his incarceration.

Determined to quickly recover his money, he decided to double down on his bad investments. When the stock market fell further, Mr. F knew he was finished. For the first time since being a teenager he felt deep insecurity. What should he do? If he were to admit to his wife and daughters that he had lost almost everything, that they would have to sell the house and quit the country club, say goodbye to friends and live a humbler existence, he imagined all the love and respect they gave him would vanish like his bank account. He couldn't tolerate that. He couldn't tolerate hurting them. So he decided to engage in some short term trickery that he convinced himself would go unnoticed. He went through his list of clients and selected the wealthiest, most elderly, and least attentive clients he could imagine and decided to temporarily use their investments to prop up his lifestyle.

It worked for a good long while. He convinced himself he would recoup the money when the stock market came back and make it all good. That never happened. In the end, he was brought down when an elderly client's son decided to monitor his mother's account independently. He found inconsistencies cropping up, disparities between the investments and the reported returns so he contacted the Security Exchange Commission. When the entire artifice was uncovered, Mr. F.

pled guilty to fraudulently taking several million dollars in investor's money over the course of two years.

During his incarceration, Mr. F. felt tremendous shame and guilt for the people he betrayed and let down. He is convinced that his alcohol abuse played a role in his poor decision making as did his greed and pride. He wrote extensive apologies to the people most affected by his scams and admitted to all of his actions. The judge had already returned the money that could be recovered so there was little restitution required. His family downsized. They stuck by him. He tearfully apologized. He completed a substance abuse program to understand his alcohol abuse and received individual counseling to explore his underlying insecurities. He took a job as an education clerk and eventually settled into assisting the illiterate inmates who are attempting to obtain their GED. Now after eight years of incarceration he is getting closer to release. He expresses gratitude for his incarceration because it allowed him to stop living the lies he had been living. He learned a lot about himself and what led to his criminal conduct. He considers himself a better person. When discussing prison he is able to laugh at all of the insanity that goes on here. He claims that his biggest revelation was when he figured out that he could use his free time here and absence of responsibility to pursue his own interests, read, and think about his life. Although he initially socialized with other inmates, his strategy the past few years has been to stay to himself to avoid getting into trouble. He limits his interactions to work, tutoring, and conversations with his cell mate. He's learned that he enjoys helping others and plans to continue his work as a teacher upon release. He feels a deep appreciation for his wife and daughters and longs to return to them. Although he is saddened by all the family life he missed during his incarceration, he describes himself as a "lucky man" because he has been given a second chance.

Chapter 6

Reforming Prisons

"The mission of the Bureau of Prisons (BOP) is to protect society by confining offenders in…environments… that are safe, humane, cost-efficient, and…secure, and to provide inmates with….work and other self-improvement programs… that will help them adopt a crime-free lifestyle upon their return to the community…the post-release success of offenders is as important to public safety as inmates' secure incarceration."

Harley G. Lappin, Director, Bureau of Prisons before Congress-3/10/2009

The Role of Prisons- Five Goals

Prisons were designed to replace the brutality of flogging, quartering, and public hanging that was used to deal with criminals in the 1700s. Back then, there was no discussion about recidivism and no worry about per capita cost. In that context, it becomes clearer that prisons were and are an idealistic social experiment, investing in the notion that men can change. In fact, prisons were originally called penitentiaries because they were intended for solitary reflection and the opportunity to repent. They have since taken on the less religious but still hopeful term correctional institutions with essentially the same game plan. Experts have identified five somewhat incompatible goals society set for prisons: incapacitation, punishment, deterrence, reflecting society's values, and rehabilitation. Let me go through each of the goals to understand the expectations made of prisons to determine if the institution has been effective.

The most modest, reasonable expectation for prisons is to keep offenders off the streets, incapacitation, but it still is not as easy as it sounds. There is much more to it than just throwing up a fence and manning the guard towers. If not carefully supervised, inmates who are intent on escape could find the means to do it and there could be terrible collateral damage including hostage-taking and injuries to bystanders. A considerable amount of planning, correctional practice, and manpower are employed to succeed at the mission of incapacitation.

Those who want to be tougher on crime would like more punishment, the second goal. Being in a prison is in itself punishing, but there are those who take it a step further. There is the Sheriff in Arizona who created a tent city for prisoners that shames them by having them dress in pink underwear and punishes them by feeding them discolored food. The legal challenges to those kinds of systems generally make them more effort than they are worth. Still, if the public wanted more draconian punishment, Congress could create the laws, the Courts could review them, and the prisons would implement them. There is no evidence to suggest, however, that this is what a majority of the public really wants. We see how uncomfortable much of the public became towards incarcerations for foreign terror suspects at Guantanamo Bay. Generally, the public wants "just punishment," which is to say punishment that fits the crime. There is a constant interplay between the Courts, Congress, and the public on what constitutes "just punishment," which depends on the standards and mores of the times in which we live. When punishment is perceived to be unjust it is a moral issue, but it is also a practical one because it can backfire and make criminals more evil and vengeful upon their return to society. Creating fear, self-loathing, and hatred in another human being is not a good strategy if you cannot continually confine them. Upon release such people would react unpredictably at best. Punishment can break someone's spirits, but it won't make them productive citizens. It also negatively impacts society and jailors to institutionalize hate and intentionally inflict cruelty on others. At this prison, we make it clear that society and the courts are ordering and defining the punishment of incarceration and that we are implementing it. It permits the prisons to focus staff attention on being professional in their interactions rather than imagining we have been empowered to hurt or humiliate others in service to the state.

A third goal of the prison system is supposed to be deterrence - discouraging potential offenders. Law enforcement systems deter crime when violators believe they will surely and swiftly be caught and then certainly sentenced to long terms. These actions are handled by other departments of the criminal justice system including police departments, Courts, and the Congress rather than by prisons. Improving deterrence would require reforming those parts of the criminal justice system other than the prisons. Making prisons more miserable would not necessarily serve as a better deterrent as we discussed.

A fourth goal for prisons as indicated by the BOP Director's 2009 remarks to Congress cited at the beginning of this chapter is to secure inmates in a humane manner reflecting societal values. It seems like a non-controversial way to manage a prison. However, occasionally the news media will relay a story about an inmate who receives first rate medical care and the public fumes over the expense. People get incensed that someone who violated all the rules of society gets well-treated using taxpayer dollars while they struggle to pay their bills or do without. It is an understandable reaction. But the public would also rage if the news reported an inmate received substandard health care or was treated inhumanely. Ultimately, society expects prisons to reflect their values by being orderly, fair, healthy, and cost-effective. Presently, modern day experts, courts, non-government watchdogs, correctional associations, and licensing boards all evaluate prisons on how well they meet these criteria.

The last goal assigned to prisons is surely the most challenging. Modern prisons are expected by some to rehabilitate the offender. We use the euphemism of "preparing inmates for reentry." Prison treatment personnel must reverse the inmate's hardened character pathology, a task that many others were unable to accomplish during the inmate's younger, presumably more impressionable, years. Still, we try. Family members are desperately hoping that their loved one succeeds once they return to society. Communities that house released inmates also hope for behavioral change. For optimists inclined towards big humanitarian projects this is an excellent challenge. For pessimists it is a bridge too far. Either way it is clear that prisons are not fully successful at rehabilitation. Recidivism rates range between 50% and 70% within 3 years of free world experience even among inmates released from the most rehabilitation oriented prisons.[14] This figure is actually an underestimate because it doesn't identify first time offenders who would never commit a crime again with or without treatment and also doesn't identify those still committing crimes that haven't been caught yet.

The Federal Prisons

Many things can go wrong when you place so many felons together in the same place for long periods of time. We don't know how well such a social system can function or whether people with violent histories, deficient consciences, and little to live for can be made to work well together. Let's assess how well the federal prisons meet the five goals described above. Regarding incapacitation (#1), the record of few escapes, injuries, assaults, violence, and rioting proves success at incapacitation. Reading newspapers, one learns of horrible rioting in prisons throughout the world but not in the U.S. federal system. As we put it, we "stay out of the funny papers." Regarding the goal of punishment (#2), as I argued throughout the book, prison is punishing. There's no doubt that it is experienced as such by inmates. Put a check mark there. Regarding deterrence (#3) this is a job for the police, courts and legislators. Let's cross that one out. Regarding reflecting societal values (#4), prison statistics about our educational and vocational offerings, our correctional practices, and general satisfaction surveys, all indicate the federal prisons are doing a very good job. In fact, the American Correctional Association, a respected correctional organization, carefully examined and certified all of the more than 100 federal prisons for continued operation. That's a record of success. Another example comes from examining our suicide rate. Since suicide reflects how hopeless inmates feel, consider that the per capita suicide rate is lower for offenders than for the general population. Furthermore, while an enlightened country such as England praises its federal prison for having reduced their suicide rate to 71 out of 100,000[15], the U.S. prison suicide rate is below 9 out of 100,000,[16] an outstanding accomplishment. Judged by how well our federal system creates safe, orderly, cost-efficient, and fair institutions, and does so while maintaining societal values, we receive high grades.

But the last goal, creating positive outcomes for reentry (#5), has eluded us. The recidivism rates, which as mentioned are generally about 2/3 recidivating within 3 years of release, prove we haven't created places that turn inmates into honest men. Prisons might offer inmates opportunities for change, but sufficient numbers of inmates are apparently not benefitting from it. It's a shame because we have a better opportunity to change these men than any individual, agency or institution that has managed them previously. No parent, teacher, spouse, employer, military unit or probation officer has ever had such complete authority over a person for as much time as we do. Others can forget about these men once they are incarcerated but for us they remain front and center much of their adult lives.

The Debate on Prison Reform

Given the challenges of running a prison it is natural that there would be skeptics about trying a more ambitious reform agenda. Skeptics deserve a hearing. Listed below are major issues to be considered in determining whether we should embark on a program of rehabilitation with arguments both against reform and favoring it.

1) Is it even possible?

It's hopeless: Criminals promise to anyone who will listen that they will change, but fail to follow through once they are released. As described earlier, even programs cited by reform advocates only reduce recidivism by 15% to 30% for a short time period, which suggests we are dealing with a systemic, ingrained problem that can't be eradicated, something more akin to managing cancer than curing it.

Programs work: We actually know how to make prisons agents of change, at least, more than we are implementing. Spending more money on new prisons but not reforming them into 21st century rehabilitation-oriented centers is like having all the materials available but then never doing the construction. Reducing recidivism is just the beginning of what we are capable of doing if we stitch successful programs together under an overarching framework. While each program separately reduces recidivism we can accomplish much more if each inmate took several programs that were complementing each other?

2) Can we afford it?

It is too expensive: Given our current financial problems, it is probably a bad time to bring up a reform proposal. The public does not want to hear about it. We are already under tremendous financial strain with government expenditures and debt. Health care, education, war, entitlements, and the general state of the economy are more important issues right now to the voting public. Why are we thinking about spending money on criminals with all of these other needs unresolved?

It is cost-effective: We can save money. Rehabilitating felons and reducing the numbers of prisoners saves money in the long run. Inmates who recidivate, have families they can't care for, and raise angry, vulnerable children is costly. Reforming prisons and rehabilitating inmates is in the best interests of the public. It would certainly save tax dollars. We could reduce the size of the inmate population by releasing inmates who need not be in prison. There are suggestions in this chapter about this as well.

The financial burden of crime is significant. The costs of crime include money spent on law enforcement, losses to productivity, increased expenditures on health care, life costs due to violence, insurance expenses, and tax losses to government. According to research published in the *Journal of Law and Economics*, the total cost to our society comes to several hundred billion dollars a year when you identify the many hidden costs of crime.[17] More conservative estimates by the federal government are at least over 100 billion dollars per year.[18] In this study, the per capita costs of crime was calculated to be more than $4,000.00 per U.S. citizen every year, which is about equal to the costs of either health care or education for our entire society. Imagine if we could reduce the human misery of incarceration and redirect those financial costs to improving lives? Imagine if during the current debate about problems with health care, education, and jobs, we had the financial resources to address them.

3) Is it worth doing?

Leave well enough alone: When it comes to the prisons, most of the public is happy to hand over the keys of the prison to the jailers and forget about it. There is no respected constituency to advocate for reform. Felons and ex-felons make poor advocates because they lack credibility. The public's response is that they got what they deserved. Furthermore, there are no prison riots or escapes. Because prisons are off of the headline news cycles, the public forgets prisons exist. In that sense, prisons might be victims of their own success.

Future citizens, future neighbors, and future fathers: Most of these men will eventually release into the community and live among us. Our only choice is to decide what kind of man we want returning into our communities. Do we want men who feel inadequate, broken, and fearful? How about men who are angry, cruel, and vengeful? We need to come to terms with the fact that they are releasing, ready to put into practice whatever has been taught to them during their incarceration. We have to decide if we prefer them brooding and isolated, indifferent and cold-hearted, or reformed and committed to live straight?

4) Is it ethical?

No to Big Brother: Reforms strike some as intrusive, mind-controlling big government programming. People are concerned about brainwashing prisoners, which they liken to communist re-education camps. The current system already offers programs to those who want it. Let inmates decide if they want to change and keep programs voluntary.

It's the right thing to do: Society and its representatives do not set out to permanently damage inmates, but they do get damaged during long incarcerations, not through punishment but through the corrosive effects of time. We offer voluntary rehabilitative programs but many choose not to sign up. Those who do sign up might get a new perspective, skill, or degree, but not make more profound changes to their lives. Even those who learn new skills complete their programming in about a year which is likely less than 10% of their sentence. It's then their responsibility to retain that information throughout their incarceration. We could and should do more. Since we have total control over three million American men for ten to thirty years we can use our control for major positive inroads into their lives. They have hurt people and wasted years of their lives incarcerated. They should be punished. But it is in our own interest as well as theirs to make the remaining years of their lives productive. Changing people is a battle for their souls.

5) Will it be accepted by correctional professionals?

Loss of control: Some worry that reforms will somehow give inmates more opportunities to play criminal games at the expense of the officers. They don't like tinkering with a working system. They hear the word "reform" and worry that we want to cater to inmates and make officers subservient. They worry they will lose control of the prisons. They believe that the courts already provide sufficient oversight, prisoners and their families have plenty of access for overview of prison operations, and there is already too much interference.

Maintain control: Idle hands are the devil's tools and prisons are his factory. We have 2000 inmates with fewer than 25% productively working for six hours per day. The rest are struggling to fill their time, lazily occupying beds and chairs, hanging around, pursuing their own activities, watching TV, and scheming. There is presently not a sufficient response to all of the down time. We need to implement a whole series of activities and spend more time engaging them. That's also a form of control.

Who is right?

Of course, you must judge for yourself. My own view is that proponents of change have the stronger argument. Given what we know about improving prisons, it's a wasted opportunity if we aren't trying. There has to be political will to make it happen. Each program reduces recidivism by relatively small amount for a short period of time. Adding and combining programs into a meaningful whole would reduce recidivism further. If most criminals did not revert back to criminality after their first cycle of conviction and release, the savings to society would be astronomical. Giving individuals their lives back would benefit everyone. Families would have the joy of a permanently returned loved one, neighborhoods would see a reduction in criminal activity, and correctional staff would have a mission to rally around with a new gauge for success. Our incarceration rate, presently the highest in the world at 3% of the U.S. adult population, would approach the incarceration rates of other nations. There's no question in my mind that it is worth doing.

The Vision

I have described the negative inmate subculture, inmate-staff conflicts, idleness, unhealthy behavior patterns, correctional-programming divide, and lack of hope that exists in a prison. There is an alternative. We can initiate a system of programming to energize inmates, improve the inmate subculture, increase partnerships with the outside world, improve family cohesion, and thereby prepare inmates to be productive, law-abiding citizens on release. We have the capacity to turn current correctional facilities into 21st century institutions.

Divergent Views

There are two traditional models for prisons. I call them the "programming model" and the "correctional model." They run in tandem or work at cross purposes. We need to develop a new model that encompasses both.

The programming model is primarily espoused by psychologists, educators, and criminologists. Inmates are seen as ignorant and disadvantaged. They make errors due to childhood deprivations, psychological problems, and emotional immaturity. They have social skills deficits, learning disabilities, impulse control problems, emotional regulation problems, conduct disorders, and difficulties with anger management. Under the programming model, the value of control is minimized while the staff is responsible for helping the inmate prepare for the future. The primary goal is to provide experiences that will teach the inmate better ways to achieve his positive goals. To the extent that staff tries to control the inmate, they reduce the effectiveness of treatment because they annoy inmates, make them passive aggressive because of demeaning punishments, or teach them to be infantile due to power imbalances. Treatment is considered separate from the rest of the correctional decisions which occur in the institution.

Under this vision, we can only fully test the success of programming when the inmate is finally released. The prison culture is too violent for us to expect normal pro-social rules of behavior through out the institution. There is criminal behavior that we psychologists are unaware of because we won't always hear about it from the officers providing supervision. We only reach ten percent of the inmates because ninety per cent don't sign up for programs but there is nothing we can do about it. As to family life, although we can discuss positive parenting, improving marital relationships, and creating a better family life, the inmates cannot really practice those skills until they release.

Those who espouse the correctional model, on the other hand, believe the programming model turns criminals into victims. They believe the proper perspective is to assume that inmates are lying and self-serving. The inmate who requests additional services to meet some expressed goal is manipulating. The inmate who wants to move closer to home to be nearer to his family is trying to take advantage of his family. One needn't feel sympathy for the law breakers under our supervision because it will be manipulated. They had their choices growing up and are paying the price for the mistakes they made. Staff grew up in environments as challenging and impoverished as the criminals being managed. Proper behavior is taught through strict discipline which is what inmates need to learn. Inmates benefit from sure punishment. "Do-good" treatment professionals undermine discipline by protecting inmates from failure. Officers wonder why inmates only "hear voices" when they are in trouble, why the suicide attempt involved so many superficial scratches, or why inmate tears only flow when they get caught. What is their solution? They would recommend fewer visits, tougher punishments, fewer amenities, fewer possessions, a stricter dress code, and more uniformity of rules. They would argue that inmates most need to learn discipline, the value of authority, putting others first, and respect.

These two perspectives are divergent and it is difficult to integrate them. Correctional officers concerned about an immoral population scamming the system do not buy into seeing inmates as needing our support and understanding. Programming staff concerned about teaching new ways or relating to others don't think it's productive to rely on punishment and discipline as a means to effect genuine change. Too often the result is the current divide: correctional staff and rehabilitative staff working with separate missions or even at cross purposes.

An Alternative: the Interventionist Model

The model that has not been fully tried yet is an interventionist model that recognizes the dark side of human nature while also believing in man's capacity for change. It is both realistic and demanding. There is no assumption that criminals want to change or that they not potential troublemakers. It recognizes that the first step to rehabilitation is containing their negative, acting out behaviors. However, it adds a second step which is to engage in honest and regular dialogue with the inmate population about changes that are expected of them. This dialogue includes confrontations with inmates about their histories of bad deeds as well as our expectation that they will be engaged in a reform program while incarcerated. It prepares inmates in becoming ready for change. It gets them to contemplate and then implement the changes they will need to make in themselves. To accomplish, it will require that we train more staff members. We will have to change the way staff conceptualize prisons. Prisons will need to be re-designed so that the entire prison experience involves learning new ways of being law-abiding, effective, caring, and cooperative citizens while not providing inmates opportunities to opt out of the training program. It is a major departure from how prisons currently operate.

Reforming prisons: going beyond shackles, carrots and sticks.

There are plenty of good ideas about specific prison reforms. They have been floating around in various ways and in various correctional organizations and institutions for years. In a N.Y. Times opinion piece, David Brooks wrote, "New generations don't invent institutional practices out of thin air. These practices are passed down and evolve."[19] Where are the good ideas that have not yet been implemented when it comes to prison reform? Some ideas are accumulating dust on a prison administrator's shelves, others were adopted but then not sufficiently funded, but whatever the case they have not been fully implemented. They die due to lack of funding, insufficient human resources, or bureaucratic indifference. Many of the best ideas were developed within the Bureau of

Prisons but not fully implemented. In the remainder of this chapter I will present these ideas as an integrated, complete program.[*] Staff members need a mission so they are pulling together in the same direction. Inmates need to have achievable, worthwhile goals and a sense of meaning during their incarceration. Initiating reform would be the proverbial teaching a person to fish rather than giving them supper.

The Program

A guiding concept of the program is to develop a professional level partnership between inmates and staff so that staff are not merely contributing to the "orderly running of the institution." It must be apparent to inmates, and apparent to us, that it would be worthwhile for them to participate. It must be available to all inmates, not just those with specified treatment conditions- like the substance abusers and sex offenders. It isn't acceptable to have only ten percent of the inmate population learning information that will contribute to their reentry. One hundred percent of the inmates should be programming for much of their incarceration. Correctional institutions would be programming facilities.

A thorough assessment of every inmate's needs should be completed as soon as he enters prison. It should be specific enough to identify the skills required for successful post-

---

[*] Many of these ideas were developed in planning meetings by this agency under several initiatives including: Inmate Skills Development Initiative; Offender Workforce Development Initiative; Psychology Treatment Programs development; and Volunteer-Community-Probation linkage programs. I modified them to emphasize central ideas.

release. All the departments will work in tandem to complete the assessment: Health, Education, Psychology, Recreation, Religious, Unit Team, and Vocational services would be included. As psychiatric facilities do multi-systemic evaluations, prisons should rely on a team of diverse professionals to assess the inmate's strengths, weaknesses, attitudes, skills, support system, and other meaningful indicators of future success. (Table 1 at end of this chapter identifies the data that each department would generate.)

There should be regular assessments on a quarterly basis to track progress and ongoing problems. Staff members from different programs and departments would meet regularly, face to face, to share assessments of the inmate and to monitor progress. Inmates would participate in those meetings throughout their incarceration to be kept informed about the conclusions and recommendations of the team.

As we get to observe the inmate in various settings of the prison, the recommendations on how the inmate could improve should become more detailed. Every action of the inmate, from how he acts on the housing unit to his work setting, from his ways of relating to family to his way of interacting with inmates, should be examined. If there are inconsistencies between his behaviors in different settings, we need to know about it, understand it, bring it to his attention, and have him correct it. If he is honest at work but dishonest with his family, he needs to be confronted with the disparities. Naturally, he will have objections and disagreements as we navigate through this. Our assessments might be revised after consultations with the inmate. But ultimately, these assessments will determine our expectations for the changes the inmate is to make. Inmates will sign on to a program of self improvement for which they will be held accountable.

While people are not so unique that there cannot be co-occurring problems among inmates, each individual would have his own set of groups, activities, and goals to pursue. Rather than moving them through packaged programs as we currently do, we need to create many smaller group learning experience that individual inmates are directed to. Primary attention would be focused on inmates' learning behaviors that would bring them success out on the street. Both improving identified deficits as well as building on identified strengths are important. In either case, inmates will be participating in programs for purposes of training and self-improvement. They would still be assigned jobs that supply needed labor to the prison but all of them would also be working at tasks they could assume on the outside.

Programs would be geared to teaching measurable skills. Teachers and standardized tests would be used to determine if the inmate has successfully learned the tasks assigned. An inmate would not be permitted to graduate to the next skill level if he can not demonstrate mastery of the current topic. Learning, rather than attendance, will be the principal criterion to judge success. Every inmate would be required to live up to his capacities. Programs would be voluntary but there would be consequences for refusal and failure.

A system of rewards, punishments, and mandates needs to be designed to supplement the persuasive power of providing opportunity. Inmates earn "good time" for staying out of trouble at present. Their "good time" in my view should become contingent on their obtaining good skills and information during their time in prison. Perhaps prison authorities would have more discretion to provide "good time" for the purposes of prison management. Other real incentives would be built into their progress and tied to the evaluations. For example, privileges (telephone, visitation, and recreation), finances (inmate pay and bonuses), housing assignments (size of rooms, features of buildings), and even institutional assignments (closeness to home) could be based on progress. Programming institutions would be places where inmates had little choice but to be actively engaged in positive changes. The consequences would be clear, consistent, and significant. We need to use all of our influence, as well as the influence of family, employers, consequences, and rewards, to engage the inmate to become active participants.

From the Greek philosophers to modern day psychologists we learned that individuals do best when leading a balanced life. A balanced life satisfies more needs and therefore crowds out activities such as drug abuse, aggression, and sexual perversions. We need to identify a broad range of meaningful activities in which the inmate is to engage. We need to move the inmate from being assigned activities that keep him busy or even that make him money, to activities that have meaning for him within the context of his identified goals. He should be able to make the connection between the programs in which he is enrolled and the goals that, with his participation, have been set with him. There would need to be a sufficient variety of relevant programs available. As much as possible, activities in the prison should mirror the conduct he would practice in the free world. It should be apparent to him and to us why he is engaged in a certain activity. Successful prison activities would look like successful free world activities.

To the extent there are bureaucratic or other hurdles that he has to overcome, they should be overcome in much the same they would be in the free world. If he were to want a job within the prison environment, he could apply for it and interview for it formally like a job applicant does on the outside. If he wants to see a doctor for a medical appointment, he would need to go through a similar appointment process that the public has to go through. Housing could involve completing applications and contracts. Recreation would involve scheduling. Every activity he undergoes should involve learning skills that will serve him well on the outside.

Since the primary goal is to improve their opportunities to be successful in the community, inmates would begin preparing for release into the labor pool early in their incarceration. They would study various occupations in a career library, take tests to determine natural skills, select occupations that matched their skills, abilities, and interests, and begin intensively training in these areas. They would be employed in some of these areas while working in the prison. They would fully develop release portfolios that include resumes, work statements, and letters of intent. They would program, train and test so they could add certificates and licenses to their portfolios. They would stay current in their chosen field during incarceration. Further, inmates would begin to identify individuals in the community who could assist them.

They might meet future employers and future therapists. They could be assigned community mentors who could serve as advocates, advisors, and a support system. They would interact with their future probation officers who will know them during their incarceration and develop post release plans that are realistic and constructive. They would be introduced to future employers who provide jobs in these areas and who could serve as mentors. They would interact with interested family members. To facilitate the involvement of outsiders, we would assist the inmate to create links between the prison and the community overseers, probation and parole authorities, employers, professionals, and family members. All of these interested outsiders should be included in the rehabilitation program process prior to the inmates' release. Outside professionals should be assigned to willing families early in the incarceration experience to set family goals and determine the preparations to be made to assist the inmate in reentry.

There might be occasion for family to participate more actively in the programming and planning meetings that occur within the prisons. For families who are interested in having inmates release to their homes and who are interested in professional guidance on the issue, we should consider offering family counseling sessions. It is not enough to develop these programs on paper. We need to support them through funding. There is a whole area of "internet counseling" that can be developed for inmate families that hasn't been explored. Families can work on internet therapy programs and coordinate their responses with inmates working on similar programs within the institutions. Internet therapists can be intermediaries who never need to enter the institution to assist in improving family communication.

The assessment devices that would measure inmate skills need to be specified and purchased. The skill enhancing programs that are needed have to be developed and implemented. Staff members would need to be hired and trained. Effective reentry programs require staff training and time to establish appropriate linkages with the community. This is not an undertaking that can be accomplished without a significant investment of time, energy, and resources.

In addition to team meetings, inmates would need to participate in regular process groups to encourage motivation, assist in resolving issues, and focus on daily living behavior. It would be another place to be confronted by peers and staff on their ability to participate and contribute to the community. There should be groups of various sizes, including smaller groups for confidential communication, larger groups based on specific problem areas, and housing unit size groups focusing on community behavior. With appropriate constraints, inmate behaviors and confrontations can have a more democratic process under the immediate supervision and direction of staff. Inmates would wake up each morning with activities, groups, and job assignments. They would get involved in committee work reporting to staff members on issues of their housing unit, work assignments and other governance issues. Every aspect of their prison experience would reflect the values and goals of the institution. Inmates would stay busy throughout the day with positive programming.

Most of us are not aware of how many skills we have accumulated through life. By a process of gradually accumulating information, we have become highly effective at functioning in this modern, twenty-first century world. But we learn this information more by doing than by reading. Inmates correctly suspect they are unprepared when they enter the free world. I looked at one of the textbooks we sometimes use here in the prison for preparing inmates for reentry. The extensive knowledge base required and shear number of new skills to learn would be daunting for anyone to contemplate. (See Table 2 at end of chapter.)[20]

The final product of an inmate's incarceration plan can be placed onto a single contract. All of the planning based on the above-mentioned principles would be coordinated and reviewed on a single document which I call a Life Plan that the inmate and all other parties review and agree to. The concept of a Life Plan, developed in coordination with Supervisor of Education, Marsha Melendez, would be the means to incorporate the various initiatives into a single contract for each inmate. The purpose is to structure activities for inmates who have good intentions but no plan of action. They might have developed plans in one area, such as jobs, finances, psychological issues, family relationships, substance abuse, or education but have not yet integrated those plans. The Life Plan allows each inmate to identify possible barriers they might encounter and then develop productive ways to address those issues. It would look like a long contract that identifies problems, goals, activities, obligations, consequences, and interested parties.

Saving Money

One way to convince the American people to invest in new projects for the prison system is to provide alternative cost savings to be wrung out of the prison system in other areas. This is hard to do when you consider that this agency has been very cost conscious and nevertheless seems to get the scraps of the federal budget. Few people seem to truly care about the prisons, know about the ways they are managed, or particularly care about the inmates. Furthermore, we have to compete with the private prisons to demonstrate cost effectiveness. We are at a natural disadvantage. For one thing, we have a unionized work force that necessarily is more expensive. Also, the behaviorally and medically most challenging inmates remain in our system. We also provide more programming than the private facilities.

Despite these disadvantages, we provide less expensive and safer services than the private facilities. How? By being leaner with staff-inmate ratios than the private-for-profits, spending less on management and lobbying, and being efficient by mastering the art of managing prisons. When there have been head to head competitions, the federal system comes out as more cost effective while providing a better prison. That is value. Despite budget challenges, we would be able to fund more programming if we were willing to release individuals who don't need to be here. Here are some suggestions.

We could find alternatives to incarceration for crimes where there are no victims identified. For example, crimes such as prostitution and drug abuse are essentially victimless crimes. Individuals involved in these crimes might benefit from alternative programs in the community. Established drug courts have already been initiated in many areas, where they have developed smart alternatives to long sentences. Ankle bracelet monitoring, drug testing, and reporting requirements supplement programming activities.

There may be better alternatives for illegal aliens incarcerated for border violations. Many of these men are psychologically normal men who cross the border seeking opportunities for their families, as many men would do under similar circumstances. Prison is probably the wrong place for them. They tend to get caught up with gang members who demand their affiliation and with common criminals who prey on them. They don't need rehabilitative programming but some form of work environment to pay back the American taxpayer for draining our law enforcement coffers. There are much cheaper alternatives to incarceration. In fact, if we register, tax, and place them in work crews where they could send money home, everyone would benefit.

Individuals who were exclusively involved in financial crimes should be offered more opportunities for restitution of the victims in lieu of incarceration. Men who violated tax laws, failed to pay federal security and exchange fees, and violated other federal reporting requirements could repay the American taxpayer. Individuals who scammed U.S. citizens with various financial frauds should be required to pay more compensation, even if it was garnished from future wages, rather than face incarceration. Victims would prefer to be consulted about these creative alternatives since they might personally benefit. Psychologically, there is more resolution and satisfaction for both perpetrator and victim when restitution programs are utilized.

The percent of the prison population who seem to prefer incarceration to homelessness would also be better served with programs that provided them greater freedom provided there was also strict monitoring involved. We spend huge amounts of money incarcerating people and providing for their needs when they should be learning independent living skills and finding work consistent with their capacities. Prisons are too expensive to be the living quarters of last resort for the underclass.

The mentally ill deserve psychiatric treatment programs or at least mental health management more specifically geared to their mental illness and less focused on criminality. Many of these individuals were incarcerated because there are no alternative programs. Many of them committed crimes while off their medications or while on self- medicating concoctions. Some of them are first time offenders who don't need long-term imprisonment. They "get it" as soon as their mental illness is better managed, which occurs within months rather than years of their incarceration.

Current research is demonstrating that individuals whose crime was watching child pornography on the internet are 1) oftentimes not pedophiles, 2) are at low risk of recidivating after their first incarceration, and 3) are psychologically different than those individuals who sexually abused children.[21] This is not to excuse their immoral behavior, the impact on child victims, their inadvertent funding of the child porn trade, or the damage done to society. However, given the evidence that these first time offenders generally do not recidivate, we need to consider whether shorter sentences, serious fines, probation, and a host of court ordered activities make more sense than ten and twenty year incarcerations. At present, our system is housing more than 10,000 of these men at a cost of close to 1/4 of a billion dollars per year.

If we were to develop alternative programs, we would probably reduce the inmate population by at least a third of its current rate. By itself, this would free up the federal tax dollars that could be directed toward prison reform.

Table 1- Departmental Assessments

Education: Evaluate skill areas such as English language proficiency, academic attainment, math skills, language skills, literacy, computer skills, academic motivation, and academic goals. Also assess the inmate's history of personal finances, knowledge of financial management.

Vocational planning: Assess work skills, employment history, prison work experience, and post-incarceration goals. Administer tests that measure personality to job requirements. Assess inmate skill levels as well as prepare them for future employment in factories. Instead of outsourcing cheap jobs to foreign countries, jobs should be designed for American citizens while they are in the prison that they can take to the community. The focus on jobs should also aim to reduce idleness, enhance skill development, and distribute money to inmates.

Recreation: Assess hobby development, leisure time use, recreational activities, creative pursuits, cultural appreciation, ability to be creative, and use of TV.

Release planning (Unit Team): Assess family perspectives, financial responsibilities, legal responsibilities, victim restitution, and the assessment of other social support systems. Assessments should be completed with the inmate, his family, past employers, victims (with consent), the community, and his outside social network.

Correctional Assessments (Unit Team): Hold inmates to the highest behavioral standards in their correctional adjustment by assessing incident reports, relations with staff and inmates, housing and hygiene compliance, general behavior. The views of correctional specialists including officers and Unit Team members should be included in these assessments.

Health: Evaluate the inmate's overall physical health, disease status, illness management, and health maintenance plan. Their physical condition needs to be continually assessed to determine if they are making adequate progress in improving their health during their incarceration. Most chronic diseases, which create 75% of our health care expenses, are entirely preventable with proper behavioral changes.

Psychology: Assess their substance abuse history, criminal history, character issues, sexual history, relapse triggers, character issues, psychological adjustment, treatment compliance, family relationships, and mental illness management.

Religion: Assess faith, service attendance, and importance of faith group toward adjustment. Consider spiritual pursuits as a means to encourage social values, such as humility, connectedness, belonging, acceptance, respectfulness, and creating meaning.

Table 2: Reentry Topics

1) Obtaining personal identification documents, e.g. birth certificates, social security cards, driver's licenses, and passports.

2) Writing a resume, especially in light of one's criminal background.

3) Learning about job search programs, handling applications and interviews, explaining your criminal background, identifying places that cannot legally hire felons, and getting more information on job application topics through the library and video catalogues.

4) Dress, hygiene, and grooming issues for work.

5) Obtaining public assistance when needed. Knowing about the following: documentation needed, appropriate agencies, disabilities, loans and grants, the small business administration, social security eligibility, the Dept of Labor and Veteran Administration, credit reports, food stamps, housing, medical assistance, homeless shelters, Aids, child support, domestic violence, mental health, substance abuse issues, federal/state/local initiatives, and physical rehabilitation.

6) Housing issues, half-way houses, shelters, renting, buying homes, and home insurance.

7) Managing money: income, savings/checking accounts, balancing checkbooks, debit/credit cards, budgets, savings plans, investing, debt issues, consumer rights/decisions, insurance for car/health/life, and taxes.

8) Developing a personal reentry plan: goals, objectives, personal support system for various issues, future address, employment, education, training, finances, transportation, judgment and sentence compliance including probation, parole, counseling, financial obligations including fines, fees, restitutions, restrictions and restraining orders, and spare time plans.

9) Problem solving and goal setting: the steps of effective problem solving, developing pros and cons lists, handling problems step by step, prioritizing, decision trees, goal setting, conflict resolution, win-win situations, negotiation, mediation, consensus decision making.

10) Critical thinking: rationality, self awareness, honesty, open-mindedness, discipline, and good judgment.

11) Modern technology: learning about cell phones, computers, DVDs, and the internet.

12) Teamwork: mission, goals, communication, identifying strengths, creativity, accountability, and reducing competition within the group.

13) Life skills such as flexibility and adaptability, initiative and self direction, social skills and cross cultural skills, productivity and accountability, leadership, and responsibility.

Table 2: Reentry Topics (cont'd)

14) Family and personal relationships: importance of family, communication, spending time with family, treating children as special, handling conflict, building bonds of trust, and parenting.

15) Mentors, advisors, and role models: value, roles of mentors, types of mentors, finding a mentor, and finding role models and support groups.

16) Intimacy: violence, public health, domestic issues.

17) Sexual health, sexually responsible behavior, sexually transmitted diseases, and relationships.

18) Resources, finding family and friend support.

19) Colleges, vocational schools, government-sponsored programs, apprenticeships, and job corps.

20) Selecting the right training.

21) Financing education thru loans, grants, work study.

22) Seeking jobs, government incentive programs, and writing cover letters.

23) Employer and employee rights, medical privacy, workplace issues, minimum wage, payroll deductions, unemployment insurance, and disability insurance.

24) Drug abuse and addiction, mental illness, medications, treatment, crisis support, tobacco, alcohol abuse.

25) Diet, obesity, high blood pressure, cholesterol, nutrition labels, portion sizes, food pyramids, shopping, cooking, meal planning, diabetes.

26) Physical activity, physical fitness, exercise programs.

27) Reducing injury, taking care of your health, prevention, and lifestyle.

28) Choosing doctors, hospitals, specialists, emergency rooms.

29) Health information, sites, organizations, employer health plans, health plan privacy.

30) Consumer fraud, consumer protections, identity fraud, workplace protections, environmentalism, worker safety, energy, emergency preparedness.

Chapter 7:

The Future of Criminality

The best years of your life are the ones in which you decide
your problems are your own…..You realize that you control
your destiny.

Albert Ellis

The Criminal on the Street

When you meet people who seem to be thinking like
criminals, their legal problems and incarceration are right
around the corner. At a high school reunion, an edgy
acquaintance tried to convince me that constitutional law
nullified the federal requirement to pay income tax, a tax he
considered a "government infringement." He proclaimed that
he would refuse to pay federal income taxes again. On the way
home that evening, I remarked to my wife that his agitated
presentation reminded me of substance abusers I've treated,
and that his self-serving argument about taxes sounded like
inmates in anti-government groups at the prison. Interestingly
enough, he was indicted about a year later on drug charges and
sentenced to several years in prison. Local newspapers reported
that indeed he had a substance abuse problem and during that
time he interacted with a secessionist group. I wasn't
clairvoyant. It's that his criminal thinking drove his behavior.
His incarceration was only the final act of this drama.

Another individual I met had his downfall linked to a
different type of intoxication- the intoxication with power.
Three years ago at a community event, I met a supposed rising

star in local politics, so recklessly consumed with his growing influence that he bragged openly about the short cuts he was taking to "get things done." I imagined he would trip up and eventually find his way to prison. My instincts were confirmed a few short years later when he was convicted of white collar crimes and sentenced to serve five years. There are plenty of people headed for prison who just don't know it yet.

Career criminals do a better job of covering up their crimes than the first time offenders described above, making detection through casual conversation practically impossible. I used to imagine that since hard core criminals were so different from the rest of us they would just stand out in a crowd. I imagined their rule- breaking attitudes would be obvious to the observer- that they would display their criminality as proudly as they did their teenage rebellion. If only it were that easy. Most adult criminals are experts at hiding their intentions and covering their tracks, making it difficult to ferret out. Many criminals are actually sympathetic, likeable people. Ironically, it is their approachability and ordinariness that often stand out. When I started working in the prisons I was shocked at how few clues emerge from general conversations with criminals. It left me trying to figure out, "How could such a nice guy like him have the kind of history I am reading about in these case materials?"

Prior to working in the prisons, I believed I was pretty good at sizing people up and took pride in it. George Bush made the same mistake. He thought he had "looked into the eyes" of Russia's President Vladimir Putin and saw a good soul. Later events proved that the ex-KGB operative didn't have good intentions. I've learned over the years not to be too optimistic about assessing people from conversation. It's hard to spot a person willfully deceiving you. When you meet a conman, there won't be some gut experience of "disgust," "fear," or "distrust" welling up inside of you. In fact, research and practical experience suggest that criminals appear charming and trustworthy. Remember, they work hard at it because it is what they do. It is to their advantage for you to get comfortable.

Their intention is to lull you into trusting them. After you are ripped off, you are often too shocked for it to register that you were played for a sucker. You decide not to report the incident because you don't fully comprehend or believe what just occurred; perhaps their behavior was due to a misunderstanding or was an aberrant act under difficult circumstances. That's why they are successful. They are practiced at conning the innocent, covering their tracks, and having plausible explanations. It's hard to accept that everything you knew about a person is a lie, or at least that you only saw the "skin of the truth covering a lie." The only consolation is the assurance that the perpetrator was skillful-someone who had done it many times before and worked out all the kinks. If it were easy to catch professional liars, there would be fewer detectives and shorter investigations. In the prison world it is much easier. All our criminals are in khakis with eight digit codes on their breast pocket. To learn how they operate, we review their files and talk with them about their methods. We talk amongst our selves to get confirmation. We trust each other's judgments. We ask them questions but with the boundaries of our occupational responsibilities to protect us. We review their histories. A refrain among staff is "it's safer in prison than on the outside because at least we know who the criminals are."

People tend to presume that others who are similar to them are "decent people" like they are. If your personality or demographic background matches up with a criminal's, it is likely you will be lulled into trusting him. I didn't fully comprehend the significance of "being similar" when I first started working in a prison but it's a valuable lesson. Inmates might have similar likes, dislikes, and prejudices; they might have the same size family, educational background, general intelligence, be of the same age, race, and religion, read the same magazines, have the same hobbies, vote the same party, and root for the same ball team. In fact, they surely know about all of these similarities before you do. They play on them to gain your trust, to allay your doubts, and to discourage you from reporting them. You never find out that they are predatory until you are victimized and without recourse. Then it perhaps occurs to you that at the core they were criminal. In that way they were different.

Given the Costs, Why So Many Criminals?

Since most people agree that being a criminal is a bad occupational choice, why are there so many of them? There are many theories about the causes of crime and there is a substantive academic literature to explore. My own view is that each theory has value and provides a piece of the puzzle, varying in relevance depending on the individual. In psychology we say that most behaviors are multi-determined, which means that lots of separate events influence an individual to ultimately act the way he does. When I ask the inmates why they became criminals, they give various explanations, just as do researchers. One man might relate it to problems with his family, another believes it was peer pressure, and a third describes his problems with greed or self-control. They are not mutually exclusive. An individual could have grown up in a deprived community, be cold and calculating, have a biological disposition towards risk-taking, and live in a family with criminals. He's heavily loaded for becoming a criminal and would need strong countervailing forces to prevent it.

There is a theory that somehow societal values influences criminality. This resonates with people who see problems with our culture as being behind desperate individual criminal acts. It could be social critics from either the left side or the right side of the political spectrum. For example, some believe that our culture's over-emphasis on "rugged individualism" encourages a go-it-alone, potentially anti-social worldview. They point out that cold-blooded murderers, like Jesse James or Al Capone, were turned into cultural heroes. Others have argued that our society's preoccupation with materialism inordinately pressures people to "keep up with the Joneses" through whatever means necessary. The media is also held responsible because they send inappropriate messages to impressionable youth.

There are theorists who argue that the government's inattention to certain institutions results in criminality. They point to sub-par schools, housing, or employment opportunities that result in poor skill attainment, alienation, anger, and ultimately law-breaking. The statistics confirm that criminality is overly represented by the poor, disadvantaged, and minority members of society who might have grown up with failing institutions and perceive themselves as victims of an indifferent or racist culture.

Social learning theories suggest people are taught to become criminals or at least are in environments that support it. Children who grow up in criminal families or in neighborhoods with many criminal peers might absorb the rules of their subculture. How would you respond if your family and friends were criminal and thought that stealing was an acceptable way to obtain needed resources for the family? Would you refuse to contribute and be subjected to the criticism that you were "too good to pitch in?" Teenagers, who are at an age where they are seeking identities outside the home and defining themselves through differences with adults and society, are particularly susceptible to antisocial influences. Many teenagers get involved in shoplifting and drug abuse on a dare or to belong. Social learning theory also suggests that exposure to violence and crime in the media and in video games can contribute to aggressive behaviors. Once desensitized to viewing violence, a person would find the leap into criminal behavior less intimidating. Yet another view from the "problems in society" end of the spectrum is that there is a form of inadequate social learning that goes on among people in strained communities. With fewer functioning adults available as mentors, the young don't internalize social rules, and develop an immature, impulsive behavior pattern.

Whereas social learning theories emphasize what criminals are taught, labeling theories emphasize what happens after criminals are caught. According to these theories, once a person has become a part of the criminal justice system, they become pigeon-holed making it hard for them to get out. It has become a part of their identity, stamped on their paperwork, brought up on computer checks, and something they must self-report on job questionnaires and applications. Inmates worry about this as they ready for release. They are required to report their status as felons to employers who might suspect them when something goes wrong at work. They get followed by the police and their histories will get pulled up on background checks. Normal breakdowns in communication with a probation officer might result in the perception that they are being deceptive.

Sex offenders especially feel as if they have a big sign on their foreheads saying "sex offender: stay away." They point out that their housing choices are highly restricted, they have to be anxiously aware when they are in proximity to schools or other places with children, they are required to self-report a particularly shameful crime to employers, and every neighbor can learn about their crime with the click of a mouse to the appropriate website. I've had several inmates in their early 20's with child pornography offenses having to be on lifelong probation after their release from prison. That means that for the crime of having viewed internet child pornography, they will now have to submit to monthly visits to a probation officer, accept restrictions on their use of a computer, and be unable to travel without legal permission for their entire lives. One inmate told me that he assumes he will have "sex offender" chiseled into his gravestone. While there are good reasons to label ex-cons because past behaviors are predictive of future ones, it is also argued that the isolation, shame, and restrictions due to labeling might in some cases feed criminal behavior. If the system won't let a person re-enter society, the normal human drive for affiliation may cause someone to pursue underground affiliates.

Some people take criminal behavior out of the realm of pathology altogether and argue that it is normal behavior engaged in by rational actors. Money is a powerful reinforcement. Opportunities for wealth induce normal individuals to commit crimes in a standard cost-benefit analysis. Lawyers, doctors, and businesspeople might be willing to risk five years prison time if they could secret away ten million dollars. Illicit drugs that cost pennies to produce but get thousands of dollars in the marketplace entice entrepreneurs. For the poor and uneducated, crime might be perceived as a reasonable means to obtain needed resources. Perhaps they are acting rationally in that they have few other means to obtain desired possessions. As an intellectually limited inmate once asked, "How else can a guy like me get a Mercedes?"

There are also theories emphasizing the role of chemistry, biology, psychology, religion, and even urban planning as causes of crime. Drugs influence the chemistry of the brain, distorting judgment and thereby reducing barriers to crime. Geneticists have found that individuals born with an extra Y chromosome are apparently predisposed to violence. Researchers conducting adoption studies have found that the biological children of criminals are more likely to become criminal, even when adopted by law-abiding parents. An unusual EEG, Attention Deficit Hyperactivity Disorder, and Minimal Brain Dysfunction predispose people to criminality. Males are overwhelmingly more criminal than females, perhaps due to the male hormone testosterone which peaks between ages 18 to 40 and is associated with an increased aggressive drive. Psycho-dynamic psychologists have written that over-reactive parenting and excessively harsh punishment instill anger to authority and reduce empathy for victims. Children with too much freedom or not enough discipline might develop guilt and an unconscious need for punishment. Family therapists have argued that the criminal family member is displaying the secret, hidden wishes of other family members, making the criminal the family communicator or dupe rather than the black sheep.

Religion teaches us that we are tempted by sin or born into it and that the devil leads us towards evil doing. Urban planners build cities with crime prevention in mind by constructing better ATMs, improving visibility, and increasing access to the police. The unlikeliest "urban planning" explanation for crime came from an inmate who said "forced busing made me criminal because it just pissed me the hell off." Another inmate on the same tangent once asked me, "Do you know why they don't allow guns in bars"? Then came the punch line: "Because they allow karaoke and you can't have both."

The view of Correctional Psychology

When you hear so many theories about causes, it makes you wonder if criminality shouldn't be more prevalent than it actually is. Shouldn't more underclass members of society resort to criminality with so much stacked against them? Shouldn't more ADHD children and more males with high testosterone levels become criminal if it is biologically driven? Why wouldn't more children of criminals become criminals themselves if it is genetically transmitted? But the majority of poor people don't commit crimes and there are plenty of honest, hard-working people who emerged from the most negative biological, social, cultural, and family circumstances with their moral codes perfectly intact. While each theory can be instructive, none will exclusively describe a multi-determined phenomenon like criminal behavior. They will also never eliminate the role of free choice in the criminal decision-making process. Correctional psychologists, who focus on treatment, insist on holding the individual responsible for his behavior. If the inmate doesn't take responsibility, they will have no motivation to change. So we don't absolve them of their actions, even when they have to confront problems outside of their control. Rather than blaming their circumstances, we focus on their values, their attitudes, their thinking, and what they can do differently to prevent returning to prison.

Should Psychologists be Working in Prisons?

In the prison system, correctional psychologists both assess and treat criminals. Research supports those efforts because, contrary to popular belief, treatment programs reduce recidivism. But psychology is a social science, imperfect and with inconclusive results, and there will always be those who argue that psychology should have a reduced role in the prisons. We get that comment from both the left and right side of the political spectrum.

From the left, there are people who believe we are "blaming the victim," and coercing them to take responsibility when we should instead focus on changing society. They see criminality as a legal concept that shouldn't involve psychologists at all. For example, they point to the fact that the 20 year old who abuses alcohol is guilty of a legal offense while his 21 year old friend gets drunk with impunity. They would argue that it is wrong to diagnose a person and force them into the psychiatric system just because he/she has conflicts with society. It can be argued that crimes involving adultery, gambling, prostitution, alcohol use, drug use, age of consent, exploitation, and even murder are regulated very differently depending on the society and times in which you live. They would argue that a behavior shouldn't be considered a psychological illness if it is prohibited in one society when it is accepted and commonplace in another.

From the right side of the spectrum it is argued that there will always be people who violate rules designed to protect property, reduce injury, and order relationships. They would point out that there is a continuum of rule conformity with some individuals being highly rule abiding and others who violate at every opportunity. Rule violations can be understood to have adaptive value because risk-taking might provide benefits to some people and perhaps to society as a whole. Those individuals who are incarcerated paid a price for their adventurousness while luckier or wiser risk-takers enjoy the fruits of their innovations. Perhaps they would further argue that since risk taking and even rule breaking is part of human nature, it's futile for psychologists to try to change it.

In any case, regardless of whether criminals are victims of society, natural born rule breakers, psychologically impaired, or free choice actors, in a humane and enlightened society those individuals who want back into our society deserve professional guidance to assist them. The payoff of turning criminals into honest citizens is huge. Earlier identification would result in earlier intervention. Effective treatment would reduce recidivism. Think of the heartache we could save victims, criminals, family, and society if we could turn hurtful individuals into productive citizens. Rather than reduce the role of psychology in prisons, it should be expanded with a view towards an ambitious plan of rehabilitation and reentry.

Psychological Insights about the Criminal Personality

Diagnosing an individual is painstaking work. It can't be done based on just a few snippets of information, like TV and tabloid psychologists do. It needs to be done with caution because of the serious consequences for a person who has a diagnosis slapped on him. Further, not all individuals who end up incarcerated have "criminal personalities." Certainly there are first time offenders who don't. I've described men whose costly mistake due to hubris, greed, rage, alcohol abuse, or lapsed judgment is appropriately regretted, such that their single transgression shouldn't earn them a lifelong diagnosis. However, many repeat offenders do fit the definition of "criminal personality." The diagnosis that mental health professionals use is "Antisocial Personality Disorder" (APD) which is defined in our diagnostic manuals.[22] The diagnosis is generally hard to apply because in addition to engaging in criminal activities as an adult, one also has to have engaged in criminal-type activities prior to age 15. Therefore, we often don't have sufficient data to make the diagnosis. That doesn't mean that their adult behavior doesn't fit the mold of an antisocial person.

When I conduct a good clinical interview, I have the luxury of supplementing behavioral data. Most criminals will not be forthcoming if you don't also have hard data. If they were completely honest the interviewer might find problems in every area psychologists evaluate. Specifically, the individual's overall way of relating to the world, thought content, mood, emotional life, motivational system, sense of responsibility, sense of self, values, empathy, social skills, interests, rapport in the interview, insight, judgment, impulse control, and substance abuse history would all indicate criminal thought patterns.

First, we would see how their whole way of relating to the world is distorted. They are not like the troubled schizophrenic or the overwhelmed depressive intermittently suffering through severe bouts of mental illness. Rather, their every personality trait naturally bounces hard off the railway tracks of society, making those around them miserable while they remain indifferent to the destruction they wreak. In other words, they have character problems rather than a mental illness that interferes with optimal functioning. It's their whole way of interacting with the world, their daily behaviors. They are continually looking to "score" and see everyone as a potential ally or victim in those plans. At the core, people are objects to take advantage of. The rules others abide by are irrelevant to them in their efforts to get their own needs met. It's all about them. Why would anyone else matter?

Criminals tend to have many underlying negative emotional reactions they hide well. Feeling angry, vindictive, greedy, impatient, and jealous they nevertheless present as having no problems or concerns. Over time you pick up on the underlying negativity but initially they provide socially acceptable responses. When negative emotions surface, they might be used to manipulate others. They may play the victim to stimulate guilt, or feign anger to intimidate. Eventually their low frustration tolerance emerges and they attempt to influence you by bullying and violence. Impatient and greedy, they look for opportunities to get "their share of the pie." Since they prey on others they are often fearful themselves. Regret comes only because they failed to succeed rather than experiencing moral failure. Emotions of caring and concern are feigned. Many psychologists characterize the underlying affective experience as being shallow. Although criminals themselves feel they have adequate emotional responses, those who know them perceive emotions that are fleeting, distant, unattached, or cold.

They are poorly motivated to accomplish work tasks so they don't perform well at their jobs and seem indifferent to work standards. They get fired or walk off the jobs when the situation gets confronted. Many criminals have sufficient skills and are even quite talented. If they were willing to work within the system instead of against it, they could earn a good living. Instead, it's all short-cuts and they bollix things up. One inmate described his only job as a fourteen hour drug run to Mexico once per month for which he made ten thousand dollars per trip. The rest of his month was spent playing video games and staying at home watching TV. "Didn't you get bored?" I asked him. "No" he said, "I slept a lot and I had my job." He was perfectly satisfied and not at all worried about his long term prospects.

Criminals have an irresponsible lifestyle and sponge off of others to get their needs met. They are indifferent to their obligations or even oppositional towards them. One inmate said he preferred the crooked path to the straight one, even though it takes him longer to get where he is going. They resent authority so telling them to do something can be tantamount to suggesting the opposite. Exerting control over such men is difficult unless you can control all the contingencies. They prefer impulsive, aggressive and reckless behavior to a responsible lifestyle.

They have outsized egos, believing themselves entitled to the best. Good things should come their way not because they have earned it but because they deserve it. Because they lack humility they have greater difficulty tolerating setbacks without resentment. Rather than recognize their mistakes, they tend to project blame onto others. Perhaps there is an underlying recognition of inadequacy that they defensively refuse to acknowledge. Wants are greater than their abilities or work ethic, possibly to compensate for their insecurities. They can be fashion hogs, hot rod experts, and connoisseurs of luxury items. They fantasize about a life of leisure but have no realistic plans to achieve it. The most popular magazines they check out of the prison library are about cars, houses, and luxury items. They want trophy dates on their arms because it's about "the bling". Most of us either increase our efforts to be successful or moderate our expectations. Criminals don't think that way. It's both beneath them to work hard and to accept less.

Another way to describe this is to say they tend towards the superficial and materialistic. An inmate who had three months to release told the unit team during his progress review that his goal was "to buy a Rolls Royce." When we asked him about his plans for a job, savings account, budget, and children's winter clothes, a blank look went up on his face. He had never considered those issues. Appearance meant everything, real life responsibilities were not so important. Money is the most important thing because it buys respect, girlfriends, and possessions. It doesn't much matter how you get it as long as you have it.

In Victim Empathy classes, they may lack empathy for

their victims. They know others feel badly for the victim, and know that it's the "right response," but in their heart of hearts they don't feel it. Even when they acknowledge hurting others, it doesn't register emotionally. Victims are "suckers" who "had it coming" because they were "weak." Proof they were weak? Well, they were victimized. So they minimize the victim's pain, assume the person will be reimbursed somehow, or at least "get over it." Employees during the bank robbery shouldn't whine because "It was just a note, I wouldn't have shot anyone," or "I never showed them the gun." Children participants in pornography weren't wronged because "I didn't take the pictures, I just sold them. Who was the victim, the paper I handled?" Although callously indifferent to strangers and crime victims, family members are also not immune to their indifference. Many criminals love their families when it is convenient rather than when it is needed. Being self-absorbed, their families' needs are ignored while being sponged off of. They plan to "make it up to them" at some undefined distant date while expecting family largesse for their past generosity.

Those past good deeds are generally more imaginary than real. They see themselves as generous while family members perceive them as selfish, irritable, unavailable, and vengeful. Criminals see nothing wrong with punishing those closest to them. They become concerned for family only after they go to prison. In the criminal's mind, a relationship is not a long-term commitment but something to enjoy in the present and jettison when necessary.

A criminal's social skills tend towards a superficial, charming quality that is great for establishing quick, fun-filled, but fleeting relationships. A joke among psychologists is that "You can't diagnose someone as antisocial just because they are having more fun than you are" and criminals seem to be having fun. The problem is that the short-term fun sows the seeds for long-term pain. They go to nightclubs and parties, meet lots of new people, and do wild, crazy things. By ignoring the expectations of their social environment and the concerns of people closest to them they live out their fantasies but eventually alienate everyone around them. A prison officer once confided that he was preoccupied with his teenage children because she was so popular. Then he said, "And you know where a lot of those really popular kids from high school are now? Right here in front of us eating institutional food." He expressed the worry many parents have: the downside of being a socially nimble person could include tendencies to rely on persuasion and charm rather than hard work to obtain long-term success.

Because they can be brilliant pitchmen, they can talk themselves into a job or out of a situation. By relying on their social skills, they fail to develop the skills and abilities required for lasting success and expected of them by mature adults. In my view, their fun-seeking, superficial relatedness contributes to their popularity while their early cynicism gives them the appearance of maturity. Without anchors of honesty, responsibility, and true caring, they betray those who like them and sabotage the trust that would otherwise bring them real success. Friends and family often pay the biggest price because criminals perceive trust as an opportunity for mischief. Those who care about them need to know the difference between being needed and charmed, and having a relationship. Criminals discern what people are looking to hear and feed it, deceitfully presenting themselves as the person others want them to be. That's the mask. Maybe they are relatively well-liked by those around them. That's the theater.

Criminals generally live in a people-dominated world, less concerned with occupational interests, creative pursuits, and hobbies. They avoid the strong and prey on the weak to obtain the resources they are seeking as they travel the path of least resistance. They aren't looking for a fight because it will demand too much effort. The only reason to go after the strongest person is to intimidate others. They generally focus on the vulnerable outliers, solitary types, physically or mentally least challenging and thereby develop a hidden cowardliness. Their genius is to read our weaknesses while their weakness is to miss our strengths. Psychologists who coach people to be open and honest might be setting their clients up for danger. Being vulnerable with these people is like letting a shark smell your blood. They are trolling for victims, or waiting for someone to appear in their scopes. Although it is not personal when they strike, victims sometimes spend a lifetime wondering, "why me?" since people tend to personalize misfortune. The answer might be that it was a random event although there might have been an element of "you appeared vulnerable."

During a normal clinical interview it is hard to get to know a criminal because he hides his true self. This is different than a clinical interview that psychologists have with clients in the free world. Psychologists generally treat individuals who want help with their problems, so therefore are more forthcoming about their vulnerabilities. That's why psychologists in private practice so often completely misread criminals. We frequently get reports mailed to us from outpatient therapists who seriously misjudged the inmates we evaluate. How do I know we are right? I know we are right because we have behavioral data, criminal histories, family reports, and victim statements to supplement the interview. Criminals lie frequently and convincingly, or cry at will to gain sympathy and avoid punishment. One inmate convinced staff by saying, "I swear on my kid's life" and weeping. Using our internal emotional meter, many of us initially believed his denials. But eventually the facts caught up with him and we learned he was a serial liar. Other criminals are excellent story-tellers who can share intense emotions of rage, pride, jealousy, humor, and joy so well that you can really feel what they are describing. Then you are shocked because after they tell you a heart rending personal story, they vigorously spring back into great spirits even though you are emotionally drained. Eventually you learn that their sharing of emotions is oftentimes just a manipulative effort to influence you or just a series of disconnected experiences with no one event having any particular importance to them.

Some criminals lie so much you come to realize that you never know the real "them". They enjoy the feeling of control they have over deceiving people and keeping the real "them" hidden. When you catch them in a lie they create a slightly altered one. They use alibis, nicknames, altered details, vagueness, and obfuscation to make their explanations difficult to follow. As the joke goes, how do you know when a criminal is lying? Their mouth is moving. Most people who work with inmates expect drama, keep written notes, and remain suspicious until they independently investigate the details. When the stakes are high, we have the inmate put it in writing. While many free-world therapists believe rapport with criminals was "excellent," prison psychologists are more circumspect and don't think it can't be assessed early in the relationship.

Insight, the ability to recognize one's own mental health difficulties is also poorly developed in criminals. They tend to blame others for their problems and rarely accept their shortcomings. It is almost comical to go through a list of criminal convictions they've been involved in and hear them try to convincingly explain that every single conviction was due to the ignorance, cruelty, or deceptiveness of those around them. Their role was consistently as misunderstood bystander, provoked party, or helpless victim. Judges were unreasonable, prosecutors were indifferent, and defense attorneys were incompetent. With such a stance, little wonder that it will take an intensive treatment program to help them come to terms with their criminal outlook.

A criminal's judgments are characterized by the same blind spots. They might miss the big picture and only focus on their own individual needs. Or they fail to predict the long term consequences because they so exclusively attend to the short term score. Often they underestimate the likelihood of getting caught. To commit a crime with confidence one has to ignore all the tools law enforcement has at its disposal such as DNA samples, fingerprints, camera technology, patrolling police officers, informants, and a vast criminal justice system. It's a mental lapse or short-coming. On some level they are assessing that they are invincible. They might engage in literally hundreds, even thousands, of criminal acts during their lifetime and think they can get away with every single one of them. They illogically believe their ingenuity, planning ability and knowledge of loop holes will keep them from getting caught.

They also believe that if they are caught they can persuade others they are innocent. They think they can talk their way out of any problem. They figure that if they can invent an alibi which sounds plausible to them, it will be acceptable to everyone else. If caught with child pornography they might say, "I was looking for pornography to report it to the police" and be incredulous when not believed. They might start a charity, pay themselves with 99% of the donations, donate 1% of the proceeds, and be indignant when the IRS refers it for prosecution. Worse still, even after releasing from prison they return to the exact same criminal behavior, imagining they can successfully defend what convicted them before.

I remember a conman, very intelligent, who could engage in sophisticated discussions about politics, religion, and culture. He was original, clever and persuasive no matter the topic but when he planned his future, he always chose cons rather than legitimate jobs. He confided that his next scam was to sell over-priced coffee. He reasoned that the wealthy love to brag so his coffee's selling point would be that "it is the most expensive coffee in the world." He had developed logos, a sales pitch, and a product name. When I asked him how he would actually produce the coffee he answered, "Oh, just go to the local supermarket and mix up a bunch of brands". When I told him that the public would do their research and discover the fraud, he laughed and told me I was naive. So here was an intelligent man investing his talents in a fraudulent product that common sense suggests will eventually be exposed. Would he score highly on an IQ test? Sure. But could he also convince himself of things that the average person knows doesn't make sense? Absolutely! That's poor judgment- his cognitive failing.

Most criminals have problems controlling their impulses, over and above their criminal activities. They might be incarcerated for fraud while having assault charges as well; or they were convicted of drug dealing but have histories of domestic abuse; or they were bank robbers while reporting frequent marital infidelity. Their impulse control problems are part of their criminal personalities. Probably the most common problem with impulse control is anger. By their own admission, they have hair-trigger tempers and react violently to frustration. Another frequent problem is gambling. They get addicted to the "quick buck", the win-loss possibilities of wagering, and the association with danger. Many career criminals also frequently cheat on their wives. They report being promiscuous on the outside, brag about many children each from different mothers, and financially support none of them. They see no problem with this behavior and seem surprised to be judged harshly for it.

In addition to impulse control problems or perhaps co-occurring with it, many criminals have extensive and well-documented alcohol and drug abuse problems. As indicated earlier, research suggests between 40 to 60% of the inmate population was involved in drug and alcohol abuse on the outside. Whether it's because the drug use led to a criminal lifestyle or vice versa, criminals lack the ability or will to stay abstinent and sober.

The Role of Alienation

While popular culture tends to romanticize the criminal, when you get closer the quixotic charm disappears and the selfish cynicism materializes. A sober assessment of criminal personalities reveal pervasive ways of being that even the most dedicated change agents find daunting to effect. How did criminals come to be this way? Is there some underlying cause to explain the distorted view of self and others? Based on my experience, I attribute much of the problem to an underlying experience of alienation.

Most healthy adults have a core belief, deep and unspoken, that things will eventually work out if one perseveres. There are many adult challenges. A marriage is strained, the boss is pressuring us, the kids are having problems, our career has stalled, we have financial difficulties, or there are health concerns. Most of us during tough times try to muddle through life using the strategies, behaviors, and ethical rules we learned growing up while we wait for better times to emerge. There is an underlying faith or confidence nurtured early on. We are not so much waiting for a particular day, but we are waiting for a better day; a sense that though one might not be on the easiest path, one is on the proper path and that it will become right. This confidence in what we have been taught and the world around us gives us the courage to pursue the right course of action, the ethical course, even when it seems like everything is working against us and we have no guarantees about how it will turn out in the end.

When I talk to criminals I hear a very different thought process. They start out with an underlying alienation. They don't have that same sense of confidence that things will work out if they do their personal best and follow the rules. Based on my interviews, it seems they lack the confidence to muddle through with right action when times get tough. They drift. They blindly turn to bad decisions. It is not so much optimism they lack, although they are not deeply optimistic, but they seem to particularly be missing a sense of moral commitment, confidence, or faith in the way the world is constructed. They lack confidence that right action in the present term is a useful response. Instead, they cynically turn to any behavior that will aide them in the moment. That is why drugs, promiscuity, criminal behavior, and indifference all seem to coalesce as a lifestyle choice.

Core areas of alienation

I believe all of us have confidence in some combination of four areas that support our lawful actions. The four areas are confidence in ourselves, peers and family, society, and/or our Maker, and this confidence provides the bedrock which allows us to take the risk of plodding along without the expectation of immediate success. We tolerate short-term disappointment and even failure while we wait to achieve long term satisfaction. The criminal doesn't have that same sense of confidence. As a result, their behaviors are short sighted, inconsiderate, and illegal. Eventually they find their way to prison.

First, the alienated person lacks confidence in a "positive self." He doesn't believe that he can accomplish his dreams through legitimate activity. The rest of us learned to establish a positive and realistic identity that provides us sufficient self -esteem. That gradual and essential process of recognizing one's limitations is a painful loss and requires a lot of emotional support from adults. Staying motivated and moral while gradually scaling back our ambitions requires encouragement from the adults in our lives. Every successful parent on some level is communicating two essential rules to his/her children: 1) "I will be satisfied if you work to the best of your personal ability." 2) "There is enough room in this world for you to achieve sufficient personal success while also following society's rules."

This message is essential for children if they are to feel good about themselves and their less than extra-ordinary skills and abilities. They need to feel they can tolerate the boredom, setbacks, and personal limitations that characterize all our efforts. They need to believe that self-determination is a winning strategy and to feel pride in honest effort and moral actions. Finally, they need to appreciate that their personal array of skills, abilities, and attributes is sufficient to make them special. By accepting this in the deepest parts of their psyche, they are able to relinquish the childhood fantasies of being the future President, professional ballplayer, or multi-millionaire, as they gradually match their talents with their re-ordered aspirations. The goals get scaled down as we mature but the satisfaction and self-pride remain. Unfortunately, the criminally-minded were not able to internalize this message. As a result, they have not been able to find ways to match their hopes for the future with their actual capacities.

Second, people need to have confidence in those around them. They need to have sufficient trust to tolerate the inevitable disappointments that occur in any relationship and not overreact to the slights that naturally creep into even the closest partnerships. They need to be receptive enough to listen to role models, aspire to meet someone else's expectations, and appreciate a loved one's praise. They also need to value the genuine respect of peers so that they will act morally to obtain it. They need to create cycles of positive communication so that they come to understand others. Criminals don't have these experiences. In that sense they are "lone wolves" who don't trust others and don't allow people to get close. They rely on intimidation rather than relationship. They manipulate rather than allow themselves to be vulnerable. Their lack of confidence even in those closest to them prevents them from accepting the support of others. By being alienated from peers and family, they fail to heed messages that would correct their behaviors. Their isolation and lack of empathy contributes to their bad decision making.

Third, people get discouraged if they believe they live in a harsh world where they won't get fair treatment from legitimate authorities. If you don't believe in the fairness of the rules and society, it is difficult to have faith that you will get your fair share through honest effort. These individuals don't believe the employer who says, "Show up on time and work hard for the next several years and you can get promoted". They can't tolerate the daily stresses and disappointments of financial responsibility and work because they don't accept it will get them positive results. Some children unfortunately learn cynicism at a very early age. During their childhood they may have watched adults lie, steal, be unfair, act harshly, behave criminally, and they concluded, "You can't trust the authorities to be fair." They concluded that trust is for "suckers" because they have been burned too many times.

I have worked with many children and teenagers who have this cynical view of society. Already young wheeler-dealers, they negotiate new contracts with adults rather than rely on meeting societal rules and adult expectations. I remember a teenager in an outpatient clinical practice who tried to convince me to provide his probation officer a good report about him in exchange for a letter to my boss about how much I helped him. When I declined to participate in his scheme, he got angry and mocked me for being "scared." He didn't trust that hard work in treatment would guarantee good results but instead believed that a "scratch your back" arrangement would. People such as him aren't able to establish the relational and contractual obligations required in a work environment because they can't subordinate themselves to the goals of the job. It's always a question of who is being "taken."

In another case I met three siblings, ages 12, 9, and 6, who had been through multiple foster care placements due to drug-addicted parents. Tragically, a few temporary foster parents turned out to be neglectful or abusive. The referring social worker suspected that the current placement was an abusive home and asked me to explore the issue. In talking with the 12 year old he confirmed to me what the social worker suspected- it was indeed a home characterized by hostility and verbal abuse. Then he begged me not to report it. He told me that although they demeaned him and his 9 year old brother, his 6 year old brother was being well treated. He figured that he and his other brother could tolerate the abuse for the next several years for the sake of their younger brother. Based on his experiences, he believed the next placement would be no better and possibly worse. On my car ride home I shed tears for those boys. This 12 year old boy was a hero, offering to sacrifice himself for the benefit of his youngest sibling. Who would begrudge him his cynicism about the world around him?

The fourth and last area is a faith in an almighty Creator. Dostoevsky said, "If god is dead, everything is permitted." Many people believe that God himself is looking at them and weighing their behaviors. Having an omniscient and omnipotent God, they zealously conform to moral conduct. Since many career criminals don't believe God is weighing their deeds, they reason that they can help themselves to what they want. They believe the world is a jungle and they are entitled to try to "get theirs" any way they can just as everyone else does. Honest individuals might believe that their faith in God is what helps them accept life's sufferings and keep to a moral course. They believe in the afterlife and so expect to be rewarded after they leave this earth. Faith allows them to remain patient, humble, moral, and determined in the face of adversity. While not the only path to moral action, it is a sure one. Criminals seem to lack this faith in a Creator supporting them in adversity, rewarding the good, and punishing those who are immoral.

The criminal's experience of "alienation" is deeply ingrained in his personality. All of his mental processes, cognitions, motivation, self-perceptions, behavior, empathy, emotions, interpersonal styles, and impulse control are infused with alienation and demoralization. Perhaps they are rational actors given the assumptions under which they operate. They believe they can't be successful through the normal application of their abilities, others can't be relied on, societal rules are unfairly stacked against them, and there is no higher moral authority to appeal to. Few people would continue to accept unfair treatment if they didn't believe that they could eventually get a measure of peace or some reward.

People who lack a conscience or have abandoned it did so when they lost faith in themselves, others, society and God. They surrendered themselves to impulses, desires, easy answers, convenience, bad decisions, peer pressures, and conflict, precisely because they believe they had no reason not to. One path is as good as the next and no one has the moral authority to tell them otherwise. They are led by their mood and wherever the moment takes them. In that sense, the key personal and social issue is a form of alienation. They function as emotional nomads looking for the occasional oasis of opportunity and satisfaction to sustain them without believing they can build a permanent home to anchor them. As the ultimate cynic they have chosen to cast themselves out and stand against society. Because it is deeply embedded in their character, they can't be argued with. They themselves have to hit rock bottom before looking for adult alternatives. Providing love and second chances before they are receptive are just opportunities for them to take advantage. Prisons will always be needed as a foundation from which the criminal can rebuild. Then, when they act properly, they will experience a responsive world.

Those who get away

The majority of individuals who think and behave like criminals will eventually get caught in a rule abiding society. Unfortunately, it seems like there are plenty of free people whose criminal acts haven't caught up with them yet. Many extraordinarily successful people in American history made their fortunes through criminal endeavors, a fact which suggests there is a dotted line between success and criminality. In the last 5 years in America, business executives from a variety of large corporations such as Enron, Computer Associates, UBS, Health South, ImClone Systems, Martha Stewart Living, Peregrine Systems, WorldCom, Tyco, Nadler Inc., and Adelphia admitted or were convicted of criminal activity, several of whom served or are serving jail time. The biggest Ponzi scheme in the history of the world hit the headlines when Bernie Madoff, a 70 year old icon of the financial industry, admitted to running a corrupt organization for most of his adulthood. In the process, he ruined thousands of lives, bankrupted charities, and betrayed everyone who placed the fruits of their life's work with him.

Public officials also have their fair share of violators. Judges have found their way into the prisons they sentence others to, violating the laws they know intimately and were sworn to uphold. The governor of New York barely escaped prosecution for behaviors he prosecuted as a district attorney. The governor of Illinois is serving federal time for racketeering, as have his predecessors. The governor who replaced him is on trial for influence peddling. A U.S. Representative from Louisiana was found to have taken bribes and hid the cash in his refrigerator. A Congressman from New York City has been misusing his office, misrepresenting his assets and lying on his taxes for years. There are countless financial irregularities and ethics probes of members of Congress. Speakers of the House have resigned their positions due to unethical, possibly illegal, behavior. Their activities get exposed after their financial or political problems bring greater scrutiny and a public mood for revenge.

I'm sure many successful people escape prosecution only because their companies are doing well enough or their political standing remains high enough to prevent close examination. While writing this book, the stock market plummeted due in part to the greed and illegal activities of leaders and executives throughout Wall Street. We are still waiting to hear about the indictments we were told would follow. Malfeasance occurs in all societies with the major difference being that in law abiding societies individuals get caught and prosecuted more often. As bad as corruption is in our society, it is more endemic to closed societies. One has to wonder if real world success and criminality are sometimes closely related, sometimes being two sides of the same coin. Sadly, it seems like the big fish often get away.

The Future of Crime

When all is said, human beings have to decide for themselves what their course of action will be. We each control our own destinies. Since Adam and Eve, people have chosen to push the limits despite the risks and prohibitions. Since Cain and Abel, hot-headed individuals committed heinous acts against his brother. No society has been free of crime and it is hard to anticipate a society that will be. If prisons are necessary, let's make them instruments of society. Let's prepare those releasing to live amongst us as contributors to the greater good.

References

[1] Dept of Justice; Fact Sheet: DOJ Efforts to Rebuild New Orleans after Hurricane Katrina.
www.ojp.usdoj.gov/newsroom/pressreleases/2007/DOJ07-666.htm

[2] Bureau of Justice Statistics Special Report: Mental Health Problems of Prison and Jail Inmates; Doris James and Lauren E. Glaze; revised 12/14/2006 http://www.ojp.usdoj.gov/bjs/mhppji.htm

[3] Outside the Walls: A National Snapshot of Community-Based Prisoner Reentry Programs, page 3.
http://www.reentrymediaoutreach.org/pdfs/health_bp.pdf

[4] http://www.bop.gov/inmate_programs/mental.jsp and
judiciary.senate.gov/pdf/09-09-15%20Lappin%20Testimony.pdf · PDF file

[5] See *Methamphetamine Use Increasing among State and Federal Prisoners.* http://bjs.ojp.usdoj.gov/content/pub/press/dudsfp04pr.cfm#

[6] www.bop.gov/news/quick.jsp

[7] Seligman, Martin. 2002. Authentic Happiness. Simon and Schuster. Free Press.

[8] Zimbardo, Philip and Boyd, John. 2008. The Time Paradox. New York: Free Press.

[9] Csikszentmihalyi, Mihaly. 1996. Creativity: Flow and the Psych of Discovery and Invention. New York: Harper Collins Publishers.

[10] Vaillant, George E. 1993. The Wisdom of Ego. Massachusetts: Harvard University Press.

[11] Samenow, Stanton. 1984, 2004. Inside the Criminal Mind. New York: Crown Publishers/Random House.

[12] Victory Frankl, Man's Search for meaning.

[13] Martin Seligman, Character Traits, 185

[14] Langan, P.A. & D.J. Levin. *Recidivism of Prisoners release in 1994.* NCJ 193427. Washington D.C.: U.S. Dept. of Justice, Bureau of Justice Statistics, 2009. 189

[15] BBC News, http://www.bbc.co.uk/news/uk-12104241

[16] USSuic, http://www.bop.gov/inmate_programs/mental.jsp and

judiciary.senate.gov/pdf/09-09-15%20Lappin%20Testimony.pdf · PDF file

[17] Anderson, David A. (1999). "The Aggregate Burden of Crime" Journal of Law and Economics. 42: 611-637.

[18] National Institute of Justice. 1996. Victim Costs and Consequences: A New Look. Washington, D.C.: U.S. Department of Justice.

[19] Brooks, David. (1/27/2009). "What Life Asks of Us" Opinion piece article in The New York Times.

[20] Starting Out: The Complete Re-entry Handbook, by William Foster and Carl E. Van Horn.

[21] The consumption of Internet child pornography and violent and sex offending. *BMC Psychiatry* 2009, **9:**43doi:10.1186/1471-244X-9-43.

[22] American Psychiatric Association. 2000. Diagnostic and Statistical Manual of Mental Disorders. Fourth Edition DSMIV-TR. Washington, D.C.: American Psychiatric Association.

Made in the USA
Middletown, DE
21 August 2020